Praise for
Luminous Melodies

"These beautiful songs of experience offer glimpses into the awakened minds of the Mahāmudrā masters of India. Karl Brunnhölzl's masterful translations are a joy to read for how they express what is so often inexpressible."

—His Eminence the Twelfth Zurmang Gharwang Rinpoche

"We are indeed fortunate that Karl Brunnhölzl has extracted this collection of songs of realization from the six volumes of Indian Mahāmudrā texts compiled by the Seventh Karmapa, Chötra Gyatso. There is enough in these profound pith instructions to contemplate for a very long time.

"Brunnhölzl's translations are both daring and playful. There is much here that seems to make no 'sense,' and yet, these pith instructions have great power. Reading these songs, contemplating their meaning, and meditating within that understanding will open doors to experience—and perhaps even realization—just as they did for practitioners in the past."

—Andy Karr, author of *Contemplating Reality*

"In this small but profound and utterly delightful volume, Karl Brunnhölzl brings to light the mahāmudrā songs of a wide range of Indian Buddhist mahāsiddhas, most of them never before translated into a Western language. Brunnhölzl's typically learned and lucid introduction ably situates the songs within their social, religious, and literary context, and compares them fruitfully with religious poetry from many corners of the world, while the translations themselves capture beautifully the wordplay, mystical wonder, and ecstatic sense of freedom expressed by their mysterious and charismatic authors. *Luminous Melodies* gives us a unique and inspiring view of the Indian sources of one of the world's great contemplative traditions and ought to be in the collection of anyone who appreciates Buddhist poetry, Buddhist practice, and the places where they meet."

—Roger R. Jackson, author of *Mind Seeing Mind*

"This delightful volume of Mahāmudrā songs by male and female mahāsiddhas—some well known, most not—offers us a window into their world of realization. Many thanks to Karl Brunnhölzl for his excellent translations and introduction, which provide us with more sources and greater awareness of the rich Buddhist tradition of expressing the inexpressible through song."

—Elizabeth Callahan, translator of *Moonbeams of Mahāmudrā*

Luminous Melodies

ESSENTIAL DOHĀS OF INDIAN MAHĀMUDRĀ

Translated and Introduced by
Karl Brunnhölzl

Foreword by
Dzogchen Ponlop Rinpoche

Wisdom

Wisdom Publications
199 Elm Street
Somerville, MA 02144 USA
wisdomexperience.org

Library of Congress Cataloging-in-Publication Data
Names: Chos-grags-rgya-mtsho, Karma-pa VII, 1454–1506, author. | Brunnhölzl, Karl, translator.
Title: Luminous melodies: essential dohas of Indian mahamudra / translated and introduced by Karl Brunnholzl.
Other titles: Nges don phyag chen khrid mdzod. Selections. English
Description: Somerville, MA: Wisdom Publications, [2019] | Translation of selections from the author's Nges don phyag chen khrid mdzod. | Includes bibliographical references.
Identifiers: LCCN 2019016596 (print) | LCCN 2019981102 (ebook) | ISBN 9781614296225 (hardcover) | ISBN 9781614296232 (ebook)
Subjects: LCSH: Mahāmudrā (Tantric rite) | Tantric Buddhism—Rituals.
Classification: LCC BQ8921.M35 N37213 2019 (print) | LCC BQ8921.M35 (ebook) | DDC 294.3/4435—dc23
LC record available at https://lccn.loc.gov/2019016596
LC ebook record available at https://lccn.loc.gov/2019981102

ISBN 978-1-61429-622-5 ebook ISBN 978-1-61429-623-2

23 22 21 20 19 5 4 3 2 1

Cover artwork: "Mahasiddha, Saraha" and "Mahasiddha, Ghantapa" courtesy of the Rubin Museum of Art.
Cover design by Gopa & Ted 2. Interior design by Graciela Galup.
Set in DGP 11/14.

Printed on acid-free paper that meets the guidelines for permanence and durability of the Production Guidelines for Book Longevity of the Council on Library Resources.

Printed in the United States of America.

In loving memory of my mother Ruth Brunnhölzl,
a true bodhisattva at heart against many odds

Publisher's Acknowledgment

The publisher gratefully acknowledges the generous help of the Hershey Family Foundation in sponsoring the production of this book.

Contents

Foreword

A GREATLY RENOWNED South Indian Buddhist scholar-monk by the name of Rāhulabhadra was once passing through a town. As he maneuvered through the fair, he became mesmerized by a young woman who was straightening a piece of bamboo with three segments. Noticing her exceptional powers of concentration, he asked, "Young lady, what are you doing? Are you an arrow maker?" Moving in closer, he saw that she had one eye closed and the other looking directly at the piece of bamboo. She was one-pointedly focused on her task, not distracted or disturbed by all the hustle and bustle of the marketplace.

Nevertheless, she answered Rāhulabhadra, saying: "The intention of the Buddha can only be known through signs and skillful means, not through words and concepts." In that moment, the three-kāya nature of buddha-mind became apparent to him through the signs and symbols the young woman, secretly a wisdom ḍākinī, had displayed. A classical text relates the insights that arose in his mind:

> Her one eye closed and the other open is the symbol of closing the eyes of consciousness and opening the eyes of wisdom; the bamboo is the symbol of the nature of mind; the three segments symbolize the three-kāya nature; straightening is the direct path; cutting the bamboo from the root is cutting the root of saṃsāra; cutting the top of the bamboo is cutting ego-clinging; making four slots [for feathers] is the four unborn

> seals of mindfulness; adding the arrowhead at the end is the need for sharp prajñā . . .[1]

Sudden awakening took place in his heart and he fully realized mahāmudrā. Recognizing that a wisdom ḍākinī was in front of him, he proclaimed, "You are not an arrow maker but a symbol maker!" From that time onward he followed her, abandoning scholarship and adopting the tantric path. He became known as Saraha or Sarahapāda, the "arrow shooter," referring metaphorically to "he who has shot the arrow of nonduality into the heart of duality." Saraha became the foremost mahāsiddha of the tantric tradition of Buddhism.

The dohā lineage in tantric Buddhism began when Saraha, also known as "the Great Brahmin," started singing spontaneous songs of realization to his disciples: the king, the queen, and the people of the kingdom. Since then, the great siddhas of the mahāmudrā lineage have continued to express their realization and instructions to their disciples in pithy and spontaneous songs known as *dohās*. The most renowned of these many songs of realization is Milarepa's *Ocean of Songs*, commonly known as the *Hundred Thousand Songs*. The dohā tradition continues today with numerous songs from my own guru, Dechen Rangdrol, a contemporary mahāsiddha.

I am genuinely excited to have this opportunity to work with Mitra Karl Brunnhölzl to translate the large compendium of texts called the *Indian Texts of the Mahāmudrā of Definitive Meaning*, compiled by the Seventh Karmapa Chötra Gyatso (1456–1539). Making this classic mahāmudrā literature available in English for the first time is a historic and noteworthy project.

This initial book, which presents the dohās of the compendium of the *Indian Texts of the Mahāmudrā of Definitive Meaning*, is indispensable for understanding the contents and origin of these teachings. In order to become familiar with the mahāsiddha tradition, it is a must-have first volume.

As many readers may already be aware, Mitra Karl not only is well versed in the studies of Buddhist philosophy and the Tibetan and Sanskrit languages but also has practiced these teachings for many years under the guidance of my guru, Dechen Rangdrol. Mitra Karl has also been studying with me, and I have full confidence and trust that his translation work here will be true to the original.

I want to thank Wisdom Publications for their openness and support in bringing these treasures of the East to the West.

May this book help all to discover the treasure within our ordinary mind of neurosis.

Dzogchen Ponlop Rinpoche
Nalanda West, Seattle, WA

Preface

I WOULD LIKE TO OFFER my heartfelt gratitude and appreciation to Khenchen Tsültrim Gyamtso Rinpoche and Dzogchen Ponlop Rinpoche for having introduced me to the tradition of Indian and Tibetan Buddhist songs of realization. Both of these masters also inspired me as accomplished composers of their own spontaneous poems of insight and realization, in both Tibetan and English. Furthermore, Dzogchen Ponlop Rinpoche is to be thanked for the initial idea of translating the large collection of Indian Mahāmudrā texts compiled by the Seventh Karmapa, from which the following songs are extracted, as well as for his ongoing support during this project in many ways. Without these two masters of both ancient and contemporary expressions of realization, this volume would never have been possible, and on a personal note, I probably would never have started to enjoy singing Buddhist songs.

On the practical side of things, I am deeply grateful for the funding received from *Causa* that enables me to work on this collection of Mahāmudrā songs. Heartfelt thanks go to Daniel Aitken at Wisdom Publications for his willingness to publish these texts and for all his ongoing support. I also thank Laura Cunningham as my skillful, friendly, and enthusiastic editor at Wisdom Publications. Last but not least, a big thanks to Stephanie Johnston for being my sounding board (both literally and metaphorically) for these songs and her willingness to listen to, participate in, and improve both their words and musical arrangements as these were evolving over time.

Introduction

EVERY TIBETAN BUDDHIST KNOWS the life story and the songs of realization of the great Tibetan yogī Milarepa. The stories of the eighty-four most famous Indian mahāsiddhas, including a few of their songs, have also been published.[2] However, with a few exceptions (such as a number of songs by Saraha, Kāṇhapa, Tilopa, and Nāropa), the many other songs of awakening by these and numerous other female and male Indian siddhas, yoginīs, and ḍākinīs are largely unknown, mostly because they either have not been translated into contemporary languages or were published in academic sources that have since gone out of print or are otherwise hard to access. Still, despite being relatively little known, the songs of realization of these realized beings are clearly as profound and inspiring as those of Milarepa.

The songs in this book are excerpted from the large compendium of texts called *The Indian Texts of the Mahāmudrā of Definitive Meaning*,[3] which was compiled by the Seventh Karmapa Chötra Gyatso.[4] The bulk of its texts stems from the Tengyur,[5] with the addition of a few other works. In its modern Tibetan book edition, this collection consists of six volumes with the modest number of 2,600 pages. Roughly categorized, these volumes contain seven kinds of texts:

1. the *Anāvilatantra* (as a tantric source of Mahāmudrā attributed to the Buddha himself) and its commentary
2. songs of realization (dohā, caryāgīti, and vajragīti)

3. commentaries on songs of realization and other texts
4. independent tantric treatises
5. nontantric treatises
6. edifying stories
7. doxographies (presenting hierarchies of different Buddhist and non-Buddhist philosophical systems)

Though the songs that are selected here belong only to the second category, they offer a window into the richness of all the materials, styles, and themes of this vast ocean of Indian Mahāmudrā texts. Thus, this small book can very well stand on its own, but it is also a kind of teaser or preview that provides a taste of the entire collection.[6]

The mahāsiddhas and others who sang these songs were a very mixed crowd. We find kings and queens, princes and princesses, top-notch Buddhist scholars, dropouts, philosophers, housewives, shoemakers, courtesans, monks, lovers, farmers, weavers, prostitutes, cowherds, fishermen, gamblers, musicians, thieves, hermits, hunters, alchemists, rich merchants, barmaids, outcastes, brahmans, gluttons, fools, pearl divers, and many more.[7] Besides the officially recognized mahāsiddhas, there were other male and female yogic practitioners as well as ḍākinīs who uttered songs of realization. This shows that the teachings and the path of mahāmudrā are accessible to and can be practiced by anyone from any walk of life—whether a king, a servant in a brothel, or a housewife—often even without having to renounce their day jobs.

✦ ✦ ✦

It is obvious that most of these songs were composed and sung spontaneously on the spot, and many betray quite unconventional if not outrageous thinking and conduct. They often use rich symbolism with profound metaphors, as well as examples from the daily life of ancient India. As far as their style goes, a lot of them sound more like modern poetry or song lyrics than traditional Buddhist texts. They do not always have a clear story line or theme and are generally more about creating a certain atmosphere or being evocative rather than being systematic or conventional teachings. Many of them use a rhetoric of paradox, attempting to beat the dualistic mind with its own weapons and point to something beyond our usual black-and-white thinking. Frequently, the songs are pith instructions for particular persons or group audiences set to melody, and as such their meaning might not be immediately clear to the rest of us.

In general, a scent of boundless freedom, openness, and bliss, paired with a deep caring for suffering beings, wafts through these songs that are expressions of supreme awakening.

Main Themes

The primary theme of these songs of realization is the view and practice of mahāmudrā—either directly looking at and working with the nature of the mind and what obscures it, or performing specific yogic techniques, especially the practices that are related to the subtle body's inner channels and energies.[8] Equivalents for *mahāmudrā* in these songs include "the connate,"[9] "the native state,"[10] "true reality,"[11] "dharmatā," "great bliss," "unity,"[12] "nondual wisdom," "self aware wisdom," "ordinary mind,"[13] and other expressions. All these terms refer to the innate or natural true reality of our mind, which is completely free, open, spacious, relaxed, naturally luminous, blissful without attachment or clinging, and full of boundless love and compassion for all those who have not yet recognized this nature. Thus, many songs are direct instructions for us to meet or discover our own buddha nature, the mind's natural luminosity that exists, mostly unrecognized, within all sentient beings. This means that within the threefold classification of Mahāmudrā—sūtra Mahāmudrā, tantra Mahāmudrā, and essence Mahāmudrā—these songs belong primarily to the latter category, though some also contain strong tantric elements.[14]

Several of these songs also contain quite trenchant cultural and spiritual critiques of traditional Buddhist and non-Buddhist establishments, views, and practices, including superficial and misunderstood versions of Vajrayāna. Thus, they certainly show an iconoclastic streak, breaking down conventional norms, including taboos related to the caste system, sexual behavior, and what is culturally or religiously regarded as pure and impure.

In that vein, the songs exhibit an affirmation of the body, the senses, and sexuality. This is not a license for hedonism, however. Rather, it is in the service of using even the strongest emotions and most difficult-to-master physical feelings and processes in order to transcend coarse physicality and experience the unconditioned great bliss of mahāmudrā, which is beyond both the body and the dualistic mind.

Another major theme is the crucial significance of the guru and the role of devotion in recognizing mind's true nature. Praises of the guru as the sole reliable source of blessings, instructions, and verbal and nonverbal guidance for recognizing our own buddha nature abound in the songs of the mahāsiddhas.

Dohā, Vajragīti, and Caryāgīti

Nowadays, both Indian and Tibetan Buddhist songs of realization are often popularly called *dohās* or "vajra songs." However, not all songs of realization are dohās. In fact, there are three genres of Indian songs of realization: (1) dohā ("couplet"), (2) caryāgīti ("conduct song"), and (3) vajragīti ("vajra song"). The Tibetan word *mgur* (often loosely rendered as "dohā" or "vajra song") simply means "song," but over time it came to refer specifically to spiritual songs of realization.

✦ ✦ ✦

The Sanskrit word *dohā* (Apabhraṃśa *doha*, lit. "two-say") has two meanings. Originally, it indicated a distinct meter in poetry with four feet in which the second and fourth feet rhyme, similar to couplets in Western poetry. Since many poems of realization were composed in that meter, *dohā* also came to be a general designation for a genre of rhapsodies, emotionally charged stanzas, and spiritual aphorisms. Such stanzas could also contain or be entirely composed in other meters but would still generically be referred to as dohāṣ. As with our songs here, such poems were often spontaneous expressions of spiritual experiences and realizations. However, it is not certain that all dohās were actually sung, at least not from the outset; they could simply have been recited as poetry. As will be shown below, the transmission of these poems of realization was very fluid and involved constant adaptation, so sometimes melodies for certain stanzas may have been composed or changed by people other than the original composer.

In his commentary on Saraha's famous *Dohakoṣagīti* (popularly known as the *People Dohā*), the Tibetan Kadampa master Chomden Rigpé Raltri[15] explains the meaning of *dohākośa* (Apabhraṃśa *dohakoṣa*, "dohā treasure"), which is the title (or a part of the title) of many of these songs:

> Since *doha* refers to "being loose" or "being uncontrived," it teaches mind's natural state, which is not contrived by any afflictions or thoughts. Hence, it is [called] "doha." Alternatively, since the linguistic element *doha* refers to "filling" or "milking," it means filling our mind stream with wisdom or milking the wisdom of our own mind stream. *Koṣa* means "treasure"—that is, the container in which this wisdom arises.[16]

The Kagyü master Karma Trinlépa's[17] commentary on the *People Dohā* provides a detailed explanation of the meaning of the common title *Dohakoṣagīti* (*Dohā Treasure Song*) that presents a profound description of the mind's native state—the connate or mahāmudrā—and how it is revealed through the path.[18] He discusses the term *dohā* from two points of view.

First, in the southern vernaculars of India, he says, *doha* (or *dvaha*) as a designation for these songs means the lack of the two extremes, nonduality, union, and the overcoming of duality. Thus, it stands for overcoming dualistic thoughts by letting them dissolve within nonduality. At the time of the ground, saṃsāra and nirvāṇa abide as the natural, native state of connate unity. Because this is not recognized, what appears to be the duality of perceiver and perceived is false imagination, which manifests as the entities of dualistic clinging. These entities of dualistic clinging are overcome by making them a living experience as the connate unity of the path—mahāmudrā. Then, the fruition—the unity of the two *kāyas*—consists of promoting the welfare of sentient beings.

According to the Nepalese master Asu's position, Karma Trinlépa says, *dvaha* means that a single "one" terminates "two." For example, if a man and a woman preparing to have intercourse are spotted by someone else, that terminates their union. Likewise, when the pair of perceiver and perceived is engaging in its intercourse in saṃsāra, by being taught awareness—the king of means—through the kindness of the guru, those who are wandering in saṃsāra are terminated; that is, they come to dwell in the natural native state.

Second, as for Sanskrit *dohā*, some scholars say that it has the meaning of being filled up. That is, since *dohā* refers to "milking," its completion is similar to a container being filled up by milking. Thus, since the masters are filled with the wisdom of the ultimate nature, they sing songs of such wisdom. Others say that *dohā*, in the sense of being filled through milking, refers to being inexhaustible. Some say that since *dohā* also applies to something like soup overflowing, it indicates the overflowing of meditative experiences. Similarly, the word *dohā* also refers to naturalness, being uncontrived, being loose, the ultimate, true reality, basic nature, inexhaustibility, freshness, and so on.

According to Rechungpa, Karma Trinlépa continues, conventionally, a "treasure" (*koṣa*) refers to a place where many cherished items of wealth, such as precious gems, are placed so that they do not dwindle. Likewise, the native state is the locus of all qualities such as connate wisdom.

The gems that emerge from a treasure are also labeled "treasure." Thus, just as the precious wish-fulfilling jewel in a king's treasure is sealed by seven kinds of seals, the wisdom of connate mind, which resides in the mind streams of all sentient beings and from which all that is wanted and needed by ourselves and others arises, is present while being sealed by seven seals. Here, letting go of the clinging of non-Buddhists is like removing the seal that is a moat. Letting go of the clinging to the causal *yāna* of characteristics resembles removing the seal that is the outer gate. Letting go of the clinging to the fruitional Vajrayāna is similar to removing the seal that is the inner gate. Letting go of clinging to any and all biases resembles removing the seal that is the gate of the treasure. Relying on the guru's words is like removing the seal on the casket that holds the wish-fulfilling gem. Relying on making these words a living experience by uniting our mind stream with them is similar to having arrived inside the casket. Relying on the dawning of the wisdom for which the actual reality of these words is revealed resembles removing the gem's wraps of finest silk brocades and so on. By washing and polishing this wish-fulfilling gem that emerges from these seven seals, attaching it to the top of a victory banner, and supplicating it, all that we may want and need comes forth.

Likewise, the connate wisdom that dwells within the cocoon of sentient beings is made a living experience by relying on the path through the unity of pairs such as prajñā and means, and creation stage and completion stage. If it is attached to the top of the victory banner of stainless practice and supplicated by sustaining the continuum of the very experience of realization, awakening in the form of the three kāyas takes place and thus all that we and others may want and need arises.

Song (*gīti*) means that the instantaneous revelation of this wisdom is spontaneously set to melody from within one's experience, without hiding anything. For the sake of being easily understood by all people high and low, such songs are not constrained by prosody but sung in an ad hoc manner. Therefore, they are songs that point out the treasure of the inexhaustible qualities of connate wisdom.

✦ ✦ ✦

Vajra songs (*vajragīti*), the second genre of songs of realization, are either recognizable by the fact that their titles contain the word *vajragīti* or by being identified as having been sung in the context of a *gaṇacakra* (originally, vajragītis were recited or sung only at such tantric ritual feasts). Such vajra songs often exhibit more ornate poetic refinement than dohās, are usually short (most of them consist of just a single stanza), and are rich in metaphors. They feel even more like actual songs, evoking certain feelings, experiences, or realizations rather than just promoting certain doctrines.

✦ ✦ ✦

Finally, conduct songs (*caryāgīti*) speak about the way of life ("conduct") of tantric yogic practitioners. Originally, such songs were in all probability sung spontaneously at different occasions, but eventually they came to be stand-alone performance songs (often with music and dance). Usually, these songs are rather short, many consisting of about five stanzas. However, they are often incorporated in a collection of such songs and accompanied by musical instruments as well as one or more dancers in richly adorned attire, symbolizing Buddhist tantric deities. Thus, a tantric performance of such a cycle can last several hours or even an entire day. In this way, following their ad-hoc origins, over time, these songs tended to become more elaborate through such musical arrangements and choreographies. The best-known historical example of this genre is a collection of fifty songs called *Caryāgītikoṣa* in old Bengali, which also contains the names of the *rāgas* (melodies) in which each song is to be sung. However, these kinds of songs are still regularly performed to this day during certain ceremonies in the Newari Vajrayāna Buddhist communities in Nepal.

✦ ✦ ✦

In sum, practically speaking, vajragītis and caryāgītis differ from dohās mainly in terms of their different context and function. Dohās are spontaneous spiritual aphorisms expressed in the form of rhyming couplets. Vajragītis are songs sung in the specific context of a gaṇacakra. Caryāgītis came to be individual or group performances (often of a cycle of such songs), typically elaborately choreographed, that can either be presented in the context of a gaṇacakra or on other occasions. However, just like the songs themselves do not follow a strict pattern, the distinctions between these three "genres" are far from being hard and fast. For example, dohās can also be sung at a gaṇacakra and vajragītis outside of a gaṇacakra. Also, any of them can be in the dohā meter or other meters, can include more sophisticated prosodic elements, and may or may not be accompanied by music and dancing.

Who Composed These Songs and How?

It is not known in which languages any of these songs of realization were uttered originally. Most of them were definitely not composed in Sanskrit, since many of the authors did not even know Sanskrit, which was the language of the educated elite in India. For the same reason, Sanskrit would not have been a suitable medium to reach a general audience. Thus, the poems and songs were usually presented in local middle-Indic languages or dialects, which are generically referred to as Apabhraṃśas. Used from approximately 300 to 1200 CE, these tongues are distant predecessors of modern North Indian languages such as Bihari and Bengali, and to some extent also Assamese, Oriya, Maithili, and certain forms of Hindi. However, the fact that some dohās, caryāgītis, and vajragītis exist in old Apabhraṃśa manuscripts does not mean that Apabhraṃśa is their actual original language, close as it may be, because Apabhraṃśa is a literary language and not a vernacular. At present, apart from the songs in the Newari Vajrayāna tradition (which according to this tradition have always been in Newari), the vast majority of ancient Indian Buddhist dohās, caryāgītis, and vajragītis are extant only in Tibetan translations.

As for the authorship of these songs, it is hard to say, for most of them, who actually composed them for several reasons. First, these songs were originally spontaneous expressions of spiritual experiences and realizations as a part of the enlightened activity of great masters and, in virtually all cases, were only written down later by others. Thus, it is not surprising that for many of them, especially some of Saraha's songs, there exist several versions in different languages (such as Sanskrit, Apabhraṃśa, and Tibetan) that greatly differ in their contents, the order of the stanzas, and the overall length of the text—it can be somewhat difficult to even consider them as different versions of one and the same text. This is due mainly to many rounds of later editing and rearranging, either by commentators or popular usage. It seems safe to assume that some of the songs as they are preserved now may not be by a single author, let alone the one to whom they are attributed at present. All of this is further evidenced by some of the collections of such songs in the Tengyur, in which many of the songs that these collections share show more or less significant variant readings and are attributed to completely different persons.

Thus, the transmission and shaping of these songs has always been fluid, similar to the way in which the songs of the medieval troubadours in Europe were passed on. That is, single lines of a stanza, entire stanzas, or blocks of stanzas may be shifted around in a given text, exchanged between different works (some songs attributed to different authors share common lines or stanzas), or removed from or inserted into pre-existing songs. It is clear that almost all these songs have been rewritten and resung many times. Therefore, there often seems to be no fixed wording, as the wording depends primarily on the meaning to be conveyed and thus may be shifted in different contexts and for different audiences. This is nothing unusual in an Indian context; the same approach is shown with medieval and contemporary non-Buddhist devotional songs. They can be sung with different rāgas, stanzas moved around, vocabulary changed, and dialects transposed. As Roger Jackson says,

> Indeed, we only can assert with confidence that when we examine the *Treasury* of Saraha, Kāṇha, or Tilopa, what we have before us is a later compilation by an editor who, for purposes of his own, brought together dohās or groups of dohās that had come to be associated with one or another of those names, names that might or might not once have denoted an actual person. In this sense, there is probably a considerable arbitrariness built in to the compilation of any single *Treasury*, and though commentators on the texts find order and meaning in their arrangement (sometimes, in fact, it is they who have arranged them!), it is quite imaginable that the texts could have been ordered in many different ways and still been found meaningful by readers.[19]

This fluid approach is also explicitly acknowledged by Advaya Avadhūtīpa in the introduction to his commentary on Saraha's *People Dohā*:

> Others explain by commenting in accordance with the root
> [stanzas] of a text;
> the tradition of people like me writes the root in accordance
> with the explanation.

This also means not to adduce the words of the scriptures of
the piṭakas—
mantras and tantras are not perfected by writing down the
words of the scriptures.

Relying solely on the awakened mind of glorious Śabarapāda,
I shall write this memorandum that is a drop of the nectar of
his speech
for the welfare of myself and those with faith like me,
summarizing nothing but the instructions on true actuality.[20]

Kurtis Schaeffer says this about Saraha's *Dohakoṣagīti* and Avadhūtīpa's approach, which applies equally to all other songs of realization:

> The reader must know the words of Saraha despite the fact that his subject is ineffable. In an ironic twist, the power of Saraha's words is precisely their message of ineffability. This seems ultimately to debase the power of the word, and yet the final lines suggest something more; it is not the written word of the tantras that holds the power to express the inexpressible, but song itself. Much as the tales of his life tell us, the realization of the enlightened state encourages Saraha not to write another treatise, another commentary, but to inspire others through the medium of song, which stands above the ordinary language of treatises and tantras.
>
> It is perhaps this claim that gave the commentators on the *Treasury of Dohā Verses* license to write according to the meaning of the dohās as taught by the masters and not according to the letter. . . . This gives Advaya Avadhūti himself, and other commentators after him, the license to change, rearrange, and transform Saraha's words himself. In short, Advaya Avadhūti gives himself permission to "author" the words of Saraha by claiming that the real message of Saraha is not in any text of the *Treasury of the Dohā Verses* but rather in the meaning that lives in the hearts of the masters who have realized the message of the dohā.[21]

Thus, Avadhūtīpa allows himself and others to change and rearrange the words of Saraha and other masters, since what these masters try to convey is not found in letters or words but only in the awakened minds of those who have already realized the nature of this mind. How this realization is conveyed to others must always depend on the unique circumstances of a living interactive situation—a teacher guiding a particular student in a particular way in accordance with the individual propensities, capacities, and obstacles of that student. Thus, it can never be exactly the same for any two people and must be adapted to the situation at hand. This is clearly shown in the greatly differing stories of how certain mahāsiddhas gained realization through the verbal and nonverbal instructions of their gurus. For example, Nāropa awakened by being smacked on the forehead with Tilopa's sandal, Vīṇāpa by playing music, Tantipa by weaving, Lūhipa by eating the entrails of fish, and Kaṅkaripa by being taught to visualize his deceased wife as a ḍākinī with the nature of bliss and emptiness being inseparable, without any substance or self.

From an ordinary or literary point of view, all this may sound like an arbitrary copy-and-paste approach where anything goes and things are just made up, even to the point of plagiarism. But from the point of view of the mahāsiddhas and their commentators and editors, this approach is a clear example of what Buddhists call "skillful means." These masters obviously had a different sense of authorship and copyright; they simply used the words of the songs of realization as tools to make the points that they deemed meaningful in a given context, for a given audience, and at a given time. Thus, the singing of these songs should not be understood as just a poetry reading or a musical performance but as always situated within an interactive mind-to-mind transmission between teacher and student (or an exchange between realized persons), where the songs are the vehicles through which that transmission takes place.

In that way, these songs of realization were considered more like a huge, common pool of awakened wisdom, as well as the methods to realize this wisdom, from which the entire community of commentators, editors, and practitioners felt free to pick and choose to suit their particular settings, audiences, and purposes. Thus, the transmission of dohās, caryāgītis, and vajragītis is about using individually adapted tools and methods to convey certain messages but not about preserving original literary documents. In that way, transmission is always fresh and immediate, in tune with real-life interactions between teachers and students. This means that mahāsiddhas such as Saraha are not just historical persons to be emulated; working with and singing their songs can evoke the essence of the realization of such masters—the unmediated presence of the awakened state itself—within ourselves.

The concept of transmission or lineage here is like teaching someone to bake fresh bread. It is not about preserving the specific loaf of bread that someone like Saraha baked many hundreds of years ago by handing it down wrapped up in ornate brocades through the generations, because after a few days nobody could eat such bread. Rather, it is like a hands-on transmission of Saraha's recipe that enables us to bake our own fresh bread with our own ingredients today. Just as there are different kinds of bread (and even the same kinds of bread taste different in different bakeries), the basic recipe can and needs to be adapted to different circumstances, resources, and tastes. In this way, the fluid transmission of the songs of realization is also a vehicle for creative innovation in Buddhism, which is otherwise officially deemed inappropriate or frowned upon in the traditional framework of strictly adhering to the words of the lineage and one's own guru.

In brief, in the end it is our own true heart—our buddha nature—that expresses itself through these songs and with which we connect through singing. Besides contemplating their meaning, the purpose of singing songs of realization is to gain inspiration, receive blessings, and evoke experiences and realizations from within. Thus we go beyond a merely rational or intellectual approach, activate the element of devotion, and allow our inspiration and openness to become a vehicle for transcending our dualistic mindset.

Songs of Realization Traveling the World

The Indian Buddhist songs of realization were transmitted through a number of earlier and later lineages from India to Nepal and Tibet. The following is just a brief sketch of this complex process.[22]

Maitrīpa's direct student Vajrapāṇi (born 1017), who stayed for a while in Nepal and came to Tibet in 1066, was a key person in this transmission. There are three main lineages of transmission that originated with him:

1. The tradition of Balpo Asu: Vajrapāṇi passed on the dohā tradition and the Mahāmudrā lineage to the Nepalese master Balpo Asu, who came to Tibet around 1070. Asu translated Saraha's three main dohās (the *King Dohā*, *Queen Dohā*, and *People Dohā*) into Tibetan, probably wrote commentaries on all three (though only the one on the *King Dohā* is preserved), and taught them widely.
2. The tradition of Barpuwa: From both Vajrapāṇi and Asu, the transmission of the dohās went to Ngari Joden Chökyi Tsültrim,[23] Trushülpa,[24] and Barpuwa Lodrö Senge.[25] Barpuwa wrote eight works related to Saraha's three main dohās, which are the earliest Tibetan commentaries, summaries, and tables of contents on these texts and are still used today. After Barpuwa, it was especially the Shugseb Kagyü lineage that specialized in his dohā commentaries. Later, Rimibabpa Sönam Rinchen[26] transmitted the dohās and Mahāmudrā in this lineage to Gö Lotsāwa Shönnu Bal,[27] the author of the famous historical work *Blue Annals* and a commentary on Maitreya's *Uttaratantra* that extensively connects this text with Mahāmudrā.
3. The tradition of Rechungpa: From the siddha Tipupa, a student of Nāropa, Maitrīpa, and Asu, the dohā lineage went to Rechungpa Dorjé Tra[28] and then had two branches. (a) The first branch eventually reached the First Karmapa, Tüsum Kyenpa,[29] and thus the mainstream Karma Kagyü lineage. The Third Karmapa authored four commentaries and summaries of Saraha's three main dohās. His exegetical tradition is called "the tradition of the Karmapa." (b) The other branch went from Rechungpa to the founder of the Drugpa Kagyü lineage, Lingjé Repa Pema Dorjé,[30] who emphasized the *People Dohā*. His commentarial works are called "the tradition of Lingjé."[31] In addition, Balpo Asu also taught both Ngari Joden and Rechungpa directly.

One of Vajrapāṇi's Tibetan students and collaborators was Nagtso Lotsāwa Tsültrim Gyalwa,[32] who translated many of Maitrīpa's works and all of Atiśa's songs in the Tengyur and edited the translation of Saraha's *People Dohā*. Lotsāwa Mapen Chöbar[33] also studied and translated extensively with Vajrapāṇi. The Tengyur contains his translations of eight dohās, including Saraha's *People Dohā*, and several other mahāmudrā texts. Tsur Jñānākara[34] translated a number of works by Maitrīpa and his Indian students, such as Vajrapāṇi's *Vajrapada* (together with Nyen[35] Dharmakīrti, another student of Vajrapāṇi). Vajrapāṇi also taught numerous other Tibetans, such as the famous scholar and lotsāwa Pareg Töpaga[36] and Drogmi José Yeshé Dorjé,[37] one of Drogmi Lotsāwa's sons. Nagpo Sherdé[38] received the dohā and Mahāmudrā traditions from Vajrapāṇi in India when the latter was already very old. Vajrapāṇi's student Dharmaśrī from Kashmir, who had accompanied him to Tibet, also instructed on the dohās and mahāmudrā in the land of snows.

In addition, there were many other masters who were involved in the transmission of the Indian songs of realization in both India and Tibet. The first one to come to Tibet sharing these songs seems to have been the famous master Atiśa (928–1054), who also composed a number of his own songs of realization (which are included in the Tengyur). However, his initial attempts at transmitting the dohās met with resistance from his main Tibetan students who feared for the morals and orderly practice of their fellow Tibetans due to the often-unconventional nature of these songs.

Vairocanavajra (also known as Vairocanarakṣita) was taught Mahāmudrā, the dohās and the teachings on mental nonengagement (Skt. *amanasikāra*) as transmitted by Maitrīpa, and other instructions by his main guru Surapāla for eight years. Later, Vairocanavajra stayed in Nepal for some time between 1101 and 1106, where he became a teacher of Balpo Asu. He also visited Tibet five times in the 1140s and 1150s, where he became a teacher of Lama Shang Dsöndrü Tragpa,[39] the founder of the Tsalpa Kagyü school. The Tengyur contains his translations of six dohās and two of their commentaries. As Lama Shang reports in his biography of Vairocanavajra, this master had a beautiful voice, so he was most probably also singing the dohās, either while teaching them or otherwise. It also appears that Lama Shang wrote his famous *Ultimate Profound Path of Mahāmudrā* under the influence of having received dohā teachings from Vairocanavajra.

The three Indian siddhas Mitrayogī, Buddhaśrījñāna, and Śākyaśrībhadra (1127–1225) were consecutively invited to Tibet by Tropu Lotsāwa Jambé Bal,[40] the cofounder of the Tropu Kagyü lineage, who had already studied with them in India. All three of these siddhas were familiar with the dohā tradition and also composed their own songs (included in the Tengyur and the Seventh Karmapa's collection). Most of them were translated by Tropu Lotsāwa and some also by Nub Tsültrim Sherab,[41] Paṇḍita Darpaṇācārya, and Lowo Lotsāwa Sherab Rinchen.[42]

In the collected works of the Indian siddha Patampa Sangyé,[43] there are seventeen anthologies of tantric songs by various Indian siddhas and ḍākinīs that are attributed to Patampa as the compiler. These collections vary greatly in length, ranging from three pages to almost four hundred stanzas in nine chapters. Among these anthologies, ten are included in both the Tengyur and Patampa Sangyé's collected works, six are found solely in his collected works, and one is present only in the Tengyur. The Seventh Karmapa's collection contains only four of them. Eight of these anthologies were translated by Shama Lotsāwa Sengé Gyalpo.[44] In addition, there are Patampa Sangyé's own songs, found in collections such as *Three Cycles of Mahāmudrā in Symbols*.

Marpa Lotsāwa Chökyi Lodrö,[45] the famous translator and founder of the Kagyü lineage in Tibet, received the dohā transmission from his two primary Indian gurus Nāropa and Maitrīpa. Marpa also composed his own spontaneous songs at different occasions in both India and Tibet.[46] Among many other texts, Marpa translated Maitrīpa's *Golden Garland of Mahāmudrā*, an anthology of songs of realization of many Indian siddhas, Tilopa's *Ganges Mahāmudrā*, and Nāropa's *Karṇatantravajrapāda*. He passed this tradition on to Tibet's most famous yogī, Milarepa,[47] who composed numerous songs of realization of his own.

Both the anthology of songs by the eighty-four Indian mahāsiddhas as well as their life stories (some of which contain additional songs) were compiled by *Vīraprabhāsvara/Vīraprakāśa,[48] orally transmitted by Paṇḍita Abhayadatta,[49] and translated by Minyag Lotsāwa Möndrup Sherab Rinchen.[50]

Munidatta's[51] commentary on the *Caryāgītikoṣa*, a famous anthology of fifty tantric songs, was transmitted from Paṇḍita Kīrticandra (thirteenth–fourteenth century) to Yarlung Lotsāwa Tragpa Gyaltsen[52] (1242–1346), who also translated it.

Kor Nirūpa,[53] also known as Prajñāśrījñānakīrti, translated a commentary on Saraha's *Queen Dohā* attributed to Advayavajra and studied with Karopa, one of Maitrīpa's main Indian students.

Marpa Dopa Chökyi Wangchug,[54] who studied with Nāropa's main Indian students, translated the famous *Dohakoṣa* by Kāṇhapa (also known as Kṛṣṇa).

The Indian master *Jinadeva and Gya Lotsāwa translated the two extensive commentaries on Saraha's *People Dohā* by Advayavajra and Mokṣākaragupta.

The Indian paṇḍitas Kṛṣṇa (not to be confused with the famous siddha of this name)[55] and Ratnaphala, as well as a Menag Chenpo,[56] are also mentioned as the translators of a number of dohās.

In Tibet, it was particularly masters of the Kagyü schools, such as Marpa Lotsāwa, Milarepa, Götsangpa Gönpo Dorjé,[57] Dsangpa Gyaré,[58] the Third Karmapa Rangjung Dorjé,[59] and Drugpa Künlé,[60] but also many other figures such as Longchen Rabjampa Trimé Öser,[61] the Sixth Dalai Lama, Tsangyang Gyatso,[62] the Nyingma master Shabkar Tsogdrug Rangdröl,[63] and the free-spirited Gendün Chöpel,[64] who continued the tradition of songs of realization through their own spontaneous compositions.

Among contemporary Tibetan Kagyü and Nyingma teachers, those famous for their spontaneous poetry of realization include the Seventeenth Karmapa Ogyen Trinley Dorje,[65] Chögyam Trungpa Rinpoche,[66] Dilgo Khyentse Rinpoche,[67] Düjom Rinpoche,[68] Khenpo Tsültrim Gyamtso Rinpoche,[69] Dzogchen Ponlop Rinpoche,[70] and others.

At present, due to the efforts of Khenpo Tsültrim Gyamtso Rinpoche and Dzogchen Ponlop Rinpoche in particular, the tradition of actually singing Indian and Tibetan songs of realization is also alive among their students, many of whom have translated such songs into several different modern languages (including English, Chinese, Spanish, French, German, Italian, Portuguese, Russian, Polish, Danish, Swedish, and Greek) and set them to contemporary melodies, sometimes accompanied by spontaneous or choreographed dance moves. A number of these students have also studied and performed traditional sacred dances, primarily in the Newari Vajrayāna tradition. In addition, the late Namkhai Norbu Rinpoche (1938–2018) introduced his students to vajra songs and dances based on the Dzogchen tantras.

Echoes of Songs of Realization in Other Traditions

Buddhist poems of realization are of course not limited to Vajrayāna. The well-known ancient collections of poems called *Theragāthā* and *Therīgāthā* are clear testimonies to a long-standing Buddhist tradition of stanzas of awakening. These stanzas by senior monks and nuns were originally composed in old Magadhi language (some as early as the sixth century BCE) and orally transmitted for centuries before they were written down in Pāli in the first century BCE. The *Therīgāthā* is in fact the earliest known collection of literature by women in the world and the first text describing their spiritual experiences and realizations, often reaffirming that women are equal to men in terms of their spiritual attainments. Here is an example from this collection from the nun Vimalā, a former courtesan:

> Intoxicated with my complexion
> figure, beauty, & fame;
> haughty with youth
>   I despised other women.
> Adorning this body
> embellished to delude foolish men,
> I stood at the door to the brothel:
>   a hunter with snare laid out.
> I showed off my ornaments,
> and revealed many a private part.
> I worked my manifold magic,
> laughing out loud at the crowd.
>
> Today, wrapped in a double cloak,
>   my head shaven,
>   having wandered for alms,
> I sit at the foot of a tree
> and attain the state of no-thought.
> All ties—human & divine—have been cut.
> Having cast off all effluents,
> cooled am I,   unbound.[71]

Another less-known Pāli source of enlightened poetry by nuns is the *Bhikkhunīsaṃyutta* (chapter 5 of the *Sagāthāvaggasaṃyutta*, volume 1 of the *Saṃyutta Nikāya*). There, the elder nun Somā has a dialogue with Māra, the evil tempter and deceiver of those on the Buddhist path toward awakening:

> Then Māra the Evil One, desiring to arouse fear, trepidation, and terror in the bhikkhunī Somā, desiring to make her fall away from concentration, approached her and addressed her in verse:
>
> "That state so hard to achieve
> Which is to be attained by the seers,
> Can't be attained by a woman
> With her two-fingered wisdom."[72]
>
> Then it occurred to the bhikkhunī Somā: "Now who is this that recited the verse—a human being or a nonhuman being?" Then it occurred to her: "This is Māra the Evil One, who has recited the verse desiring to arouse fear, trepidation, and terror in me, desiring to make me fall away from concentration."
>
> Then the bhikkhunī Somā, having understood, "This is Māra the Evil One," replied to him in verses:
>
> "What does womanhood matter at all
> When the mind is concentrated well,
> When knowledge flows on steadily
> As one sees correctly into Dhamma.
>
> "One to whom it might occur,
> 'I'm a woman' or 'I'm a man'
> Or 'I'm anything at all'—
> Is fit for Māra to address."
>
> Then Māra the Evil One, realizing, "The bhikkhunī Somā knows me," sad and disappointed, disappeared right there.[73]

The Mahāyāna schools also abound with many poems of awakened wisdom. For example, Candrakīrti's *Entering the Prajñā of Madhyamaka* says,

> There is neither seeming nor ultimate
> There is neither buddha nor sentient being
>
> There is neither view nor meditation
> There is neither conduct nor fruition—
> familiarize with the actuality of this!
> Let mind free of thoughts be in its own peace!
>
> Without anything to identify, without distraction,
> Without characteristics, and lucid—thus meditate![74]

Atiśa's *Song of Beholding the Dharmadhātu* states,

> Hence, the defining characteristic of mind
> is established as being self-awareness
> Since suchness is hard to realize,
> its nature cannot be represented
>
> Since this self-awareness is subtle,
> it is seen by the buddhas' subtle seeing
> Though it dwells within us, someone like me
> does not see it by virtue of ignorance[75]

As a genre, Buddhist songs of realization share a common background with Jain Apabhraṃśa works and medieval Indian devotional poetry in Hindi, Marathi, Punjabi, Kashmiri, Bengali, and other languages. Many of these compositions continue to be sung as part of lively traditions in India today, such as among the Bāuls and the Kartābhajās in Bengal. The most famous among the many saints in these traditions—revered by Hindus, Jains, and Sufis alike—is the Indian poet-saint Kabīr (1440–1518), who said the following:

The mind is a nervous thief.
The mind is a pure cheat.
The ruin of sages, men, and gods,
the mind has a thousand gates.[76]

As far as the spontaneous composition, the iconoclastic tendencies, and the transcendence of ordinary thinking and the dualistic mind go, Buddhist songs of realization also have some parallels in a number of other forms of poetry, mystical revelations in different spiritual traditions, and even some contemporary genres of music with their spontaneous lyrics. Examples include the works of the Chinese poet Han Shan (ca. 800 CE), the Persian poet Rumi (1207–1273), the German mystic Meister Eckhart (1260–1327), the Spanish saint San Juan de la Cruz (St. John of the Cross; 1542–1591), the English poet William Blake (1757–1827), and the American Beat poets Jack Kerouac (1922–1969) and Allen Ginsberg (1926–1997), as well as Japanese haikus and koans throughout the centuries and modern musical genres such as blues, gospel, rap, and hip-hop in their raw, noncommercialized forms, to mention just a few.

Let's begin with the Catholic theologian, philosopher, and mystic Meister Eckhart:

God is always ready,
but we are very unready
God is very close to us,
but we are distant from him
God is inside,
but we are outside
God has his home within us,
but we are strangers

An anecdote about Meister Eckhart goes like this:

Meister Eckhart met a handsome naked boy. He asked him where he came from. "I come from God." "Where did you leave him?" "In hearts with virtue." "Where do you go?" "To God." "Where do you find him?" "Where I left all creatures." "Who are you?" "A king." "Where is your kingdom?" "In my heart." "Be careful so that nobody shares it with you!" "I do so." Meister Eckhart led the boy to his cell and said, "Take any garment you wish." The boy said, "Then I wouldn't be a king" and disappeared. He had been God himself pulling Meister Eckhart's leg.[77]

William Blake ventured,

Man was made for Joy and Woe
And when this we rightly know
Thro' the world we safely go,
Joy and Woe are woven fine,

A clothing for the Soul divine:
Under every grief and pine
Runs a joy with silken twine.[78]

Influenced by Buddhist thought, Jack Kerouac's *Form in the Norm* states,

Instead of bothering with either one side of the coin
or the other, throw it away—in the same way,
instead of bothering with either arbitrary conception
of manifested phenomena or non-manifested non-
        phenomena,
the coin of existence,
throw it away—
Rest beyond conception.[79]

In his poem *Father Death Blues*, Allen Ginsberg reflected on the death of his beloved father and also included an homage to his guru, Chögyam Trungpa Rinpoche (in the second three-line stanza below):

Guru Death your words are true
Teacher Death I do thank you
For inspiring me to sing this Blues

> Buddha Death, I wake with you
> Dharma Death, your mind is new
> Sangha Death, we'll work it through[80]

Bruce Springsteen says this about the blues:

> You can sing about your misery, the whole world's misery, your most devastating experience, but there is something in the gathering of souls that blows the blues away. Something that lets some sun in, that keeps you breathing, that lifts you in a way that can't be explained, only experienced.[81]

The hip-hop group Arrested Development sings this in the song "Ease My Mind":

> Mind and soul is even more important than body
> Well, you can put my body in all exotic spaces
> Meanwhile my mind, it so remotely dwells
> within that fine spot between all f---ed up and hell
> . . .
> Give me a face pencil to draw a smile on me
> . . .
> And say my prayer to give my earthly body inner, inner peace
> until that day upon which my soul's released

About the Songs in This Book

The sixty-one songs selected in this volume include compositions by both male and female mahāsiddhas, yogīs, yoginīs, and ḍākinīs (generally, names ending in *-ā* or *-ī* are those of women). The composers include a king attached to his flower garden, a princess whose spiritual sincerity converted her non-Buddhist husband, top-notch Buddhist scholars (some who were part of the Buddhist establishment and some who had dropped out), two housewives who chopped off their heads as signs of accomplishment, a narcissistic bodybuilder, a shoemaker, ḍākinīs with fanciful names, a weaver, a tribal hunter, an alchemist, a conman, a musician engrossed in his music, a siddha who loved his dog more than being in a heavenly paradise, an archer, practitioners deliberately acting like lunatics, a siddha riding a pregnant tigress, and a whole choir of ḍākinīs. Their songs range from summaries of mahāmudrā and the entire path of realizing it to pithy four-liners that point their finger directly at the buddha within us. What is common to all of them is the message of introducing us to mahāmudrā—mind's innate unity of luminosity and awareness that does not know any birth, death, or suffering.

Most of the songs included here have never been translated into any language other than Tibetan. I have deliberately omitted source references, Tibetan texts, comments, critical apparatuses, and footnotes because this small collection is intended for a general audience. For all such details and more information on the background, the fluid nature, and the transmission of dohās, vajragītis, and caryāgītis within India and Tibet, see Jackson (2004) and Schaeffer (2005), as well as the introduction to my forthcoming translation of the Seventh Karmapa's collection of Indian Mahāmudrā texts.[82]

May this book be considered a small and humble contribution to the living tradition of Buddhist songs of realization. May the poems here inspire and be of benefit to countless beings. May they realize what these songs sing about—mind's true nature of great bliss beyond any clinging or suffering.

Sarva maṅgalaṃ—May everything be auspicious!

Translations

A Synopsis of Mahāmudrā by Nāropa, the erudite dropout

I pay homage within the natural state of great bliss

Here's what is to be expressed as mahāmudrā:
All phenomena are your own mind
Seeing outer objects is the deluded mind—
they are like dreams—empty of essence [1]

Mind is the sheer movement of discursive awareness,
lacking a nature of its own, the display of the vāyus
It is empty of any essence, similar to space
All phenomena abide equally, just like space [2]

What is expressed as "mahāmudrā"
cannot be shown through its own essence
Therefore, the suchness of mind
is the very state of mahāmudrā [3]

It cannot be contrived or changed
If someone sees and realizes this true reality,
all that can possibly appear is mahāmudrā—
simply the great, all-encompassing dharmakāya [4]

Letting this nature be, loose and without contrivance,
it cannot be conceived—the dharmakāya
If it is let be without searching, that is meditation—
meditating while searching is the deluded mind [5]

Just as with space and its miraculous displays,
as there is neither meditation nor nonmeditation,
how could there be separation or nonseparation?
Yogīs realize that it is just this way [6]

All actions that are virtues and wrongdoings
will be free by knowing this true reality
The afflictions are great wisdom
as with a forest fire, they are the yogī's aids [7]

How could there exist a time of going or staying?
What about dhyāna if you have gone to a hermitage?
Except just temporarily, you will not become free
without realizing true reality, no matter through what [8]

If true reality is realized, what is it that binds?
Apart from remaining undistractedly in the natural state,
there is nothing to fix or to meditate on with a remedy
in the sense of "resting in meditative equipoise" or "not resting" [9]

In this, there isn't anything at all that is established
Appearances free in themselves are the dharmadhātu
Thoughts free in themselves are great wisdom
The equality of nonduality is the dharmakāya [10]

Like the steady flow of a great river,
however you may behave, it is meaningful
This is the buddhahood that is everlasting—
great bliss without any place for saṃsāra [11]

Phenomena are empty of their own essence
The mind that clings to being empty is pure in its own place
This mental nonengagement free of mind
constitutes the path of all buddhas [12]

For the most fortunate ones,
I put my heartfelt advice into words
Through this, may every single being
come to abide in mahāmudrā [13]

A song by the ḍākinī Tuft Topknot

Hey! If there is no duality, there is no bondage or freedom
If there is nothing to identify, there are no obscurations
If there is no self and other, there is no desire or hatred
If there is nothing to mind, there is no distraction

A song by Tantipa, the weaver of the garb of awakening

Those weavers in the world
are weaving all kinds of yarns
I, through the guru's pith instructions,
weave the entirety of phenomena [1]

With the emptiness of the five wisdoms
as my yarn, the pith instructions as my comb,
and the loom of prajñā as well,
I weave the nonduality of expanse and awareness
        into the dharmakāya [2]

Five Stanzas on the Love Between Means and Prajñā by Maitrīpa, the fusionist of Mahāmudrā and Madhyamaka

I pay homage to glorious Vajrasattva

Were it not for the adorable bridegroom
of appearance as mere dependent origination,
the impassioned bride of emptiness
would be no better than dead [1]

Emptiness is the most lovely bride,
a ravishing beauty beyond compare
If he ever became separated from her,
that handsome bridegroom would be crushed [2]

Therefore, trembling with anxiety,
bride and bridegroom approach the guru
Through their inborn pleasure,
he turns it into connate love [3]

AHO! The genuine guru's sagacity
and great skill are so wonderful
The two are indivisible from the native state,
nonreferential, and unsurpassable [4]

With all characteristics complete
and free of the two extremes,
this couple is the nature of all that is
but always manifests without a nature[83] [5]

A song by the ḍākinī Queen of Splendor

Don't be distracted from where there is nothing to mind!
Saṃsāra by virtue of distraction is similar to a dream
If realized, this is like a person waking up from sleep
As far as I am concerned, I have not seen any saṃsāra

A Pith Instruction on Mahāmudrā (*Ganges Mahāmudrā*) by Tilopa, the self-awakened one

I pay homage to glorious connateness

Though mahāmudrā cannot be taught,
working with hardship and having respect for the guru,
you endure suffering, oh insightful Nāropa
You fortunate one, take the following to heart! [1]

Hey, take a good look at the world's phenomena!
Unable to persist, they are like dreams and illusions
Dreams and illusions do not exist in actuality
Hence, be weary and cast off worldly activities! [2]

Sever all attachment and aversion toward retinues, places, and relatives!
Meditate alone in forests, mountain retreats, and hermitages!
Rest in the natural state of there being nothing to meditate!
If you attain the unattainable, you have attained mahāmudrā [3]

Saṃsāra's phenomena are meaningless—the causes of suffering
Since created phenomena lack any pith, behold the ultimate pith!

Through mind's phenomena, the actuality beyond mind is not seen
Through the phenomena of doing, the actuality of nothing to be done is not found [4]

If you wish to attain the actuality of nothing to be done that's beyond mind,
cut to the root of your own mind and let awareness nakedly be!
Allow the polluted waters of thoughts to become clear!
Do not stop or make up appearances, let them be in their own seat!
If there is no rejecting or adopting, this is to be free as mahāmudrā [5]

Take the example of a lush tree with its trunk, branches, leaves, and petals—
once its root is severed, its billions of branches and leaves will wither
Take the example of darkness gathered over thousands of eons—
a single lamp will dispel the accumulation of this gloom
Likewise, a single moment of your own mind's luminosity
dispels all wrongdoings and obscurations amassed for eons [6]

If persons with lesser insight cannot rest in this actuality,
they seize the vāyus' key points and get to awareness's core
Through many gazing techniques and ways to hold the mind,
they apply themselves until awareness rests in its natural state [7]

For example, if the center of the sky is examined,
any grasping at a middle and an end will cease
Likewise, if the mind is examining the mind,
the hosts of thoughts cease, leaving a resting free of thoughts
Thus, mind's nature—unsurpassable awakening—is seen [8]

Take the example of clouds due to vapor on earth vanishing in the sky—
they neither go anywhere, nor do they dwell anywhere
The same goes for the hosts of thoughts sprung from the mind—
by seeing your own mind, the waves of its thoughts ebb away [9]

Take the example of space beyond any color or shape—
it is untainted and unchangeable by black or white
Likewise, your own mind transcends color and shape,
untainted by any black or white phenomena of virtue or evil [10]

Take the example of the clear and pure heart of the sun—
it is not obscured by the darkness of a thousand eons
Likewise, the luminous heart of your own mind
cannot be obscured by saṃsāra with all its eons [11]

As an example, space may conventionally be labeled as empty,
but space cannot really be described as being like this
Likewise, though your own mind may be expressed as "luminosity,"
there is no basis for designating it as being established as such
through that expression [12]

For example, which space is supported by which?
Likewise, your own mind, mahāmudrā, lacks any supporting ground
Relax in the uncontrived native state and let it be! [13]

Having relaxed tightness, there is no doubt about being free
Thus, the nature of the mind resembles space—
there's not a single phenomenon not included in it [14]

Dropping all bodily activity, let be in naturalness!
Let your speech be without saying much, like an echo!
Don't think in your mind, behold the dharma of the final leap! [15]

Since the body is without any pith, it is just like a bamboo cane
Mind is like the center of space, beyond any object of thinking
Without letting it wander or settling it, relax and let it be in its
natural state! [16]

If mind is without any point to be directed to, this is mahāmudrā
By being familiar with this, unsurpassable awakening is attained

Without any object of focus, the nature of the mind is lucid
Without any path to travel, the first step on the path to buddhahood is taken
By being familiar with nothing to meditate on, unsurpassable awakening is attained [17]

Transcending all that perceives and is perceived is the king of the view
If there is no distraction, this is the king of meditation
If there is no activity or effort, this is the king of conduct
If there is no hope or fear, the fruition is revealed [18]

The unborn ground of all is free of latent tendencies, obscurations, and veils
Don't create an equipoise and a thereafter, let be in the unborn essence!
Appearances are self-appearances, mind's phenomena are exhausted [19]

Complete freedom from extremes is the supreme king of the view
Boundless and spacious depth is the supreme king of meditation
Self-abiding without anything to be done is the supreme king of conduct
Self-abiding without any hopes is the supreme king of fruition [20]

In beginners, this resembles the water in a gorge
In between, it's the gentle flow of the Ganges river
Finally, all inlets meet like a mother and her child [21]

Be it dharmas such as what is stated in mantra,
what is said in the pāramitā, the vinaya collection,
or in your own individual scriptures and philosophical systems,
luminous mahāmudrā will not be seen through any of these [22]

Not engaging mentally and free of all wanting,
self-arising is self-settling, like waves on water
Through the arising of wanting, luminosity is not seen but obscured [23]

Through vows kept by thoughts, you fall away from *samaya*'s
actuality
If you don't transgress the actuality of not abiding and not focusing,
you won't ruin samaya, which is the lamp in the darkness
If you are free of all wanting and don't dwell in extremes,
you will see all dharmas of the scriptural collections without
exception [24]

If you let yourself fuse with this actuality, you are freed from
saṃsāra's dungeon
Resting in equipoise in this actuality burns ignorance, wrongdoing,
and obscurations
This is what is declared to be "the lamp of the teachings" [25]

Foolish people who have no faith in this actuality
end up always being carried away by the river of saṃsāra
How pitiful is their unbearable suffering in the miserable realms!
You who wish to be liberated from suffering, rely on skillful gurus!
Through the entering of their blessings, your own mind will be free [26]

If you rely on a karmamudrā, blissful-empty wisdom dawns
Blessing means and prajña, enter into union!
Let it descend slowly, gather it, pull it back up,
guide it to its places, and let it pervade the body!
Without clinging to this, blissful-empty wisdom dawns [27]

You will be of long life, without white hair, and will flourish like
the moon
Your complexion will be radiant, and you will be as powerful as
a lion
You will swiftly attain the common siddhis and fuse with the
supreme [28]

May this instruction on the essential points of mahāmudrā
dwell in the hearts of fortunate beings! [29]

A song by the ḍākinī Blazing One with a Garland of Lightning

Looking but not seeing—that's my eye
Thinking but not minding—that's my mind
Speaking but not expressing—that's my tongue
Traveling but not going—that's my path

A song by Cāmāripa, the dharmakāya cobbler

With this leather of thoughts and characteristics
on the mold of the vajra of emptiness,
the continuous thread of relinquishing the eight dharmas,
and the awl of the experience of prajñā, I stitch
Making the effortless shoe of the dharmakāya,
Cāmāripa is the supreme shoemaker

Twelve Stanzas of Pith Instructions by Saraha, the great brahman archer

I pay homage to glorious Vajrasattva

Bodhicitta constitutes peace
Those who are resting in it
will be peaceful, like the sky
Through what arises from body, speech, and mind,
there is not the slightest change in that [1]

Going beyond correct wisdom,
nonconceptuality will be peace
Thoughts being at peace is buddhahood—
exactly this is the knowledge of all aspects [2]

Seeing the true state as the true state,
any of the thoughts that thus arise
represent nonconceptual wisdom,
since distinct fluxes are perceived [3]

The nature of all entities
is individually present in all
In terms of their particulars,
there is no pride and no oblivion [4]

How about the clinging to an entity
that's a single part of that as a self?

It is the nature of animals and such
I shall explain the essence of that
which arises from just a single part
You must seize it with a perfect mind! [5]

Tigers are dwelling in caves
and frogs in the great empty
Cats make their hairs stand on end
Cattle and so on shake their bodies
Snakes are going without food
Birds are flying through the sky [6]

Fireflies are emitting light
Camels summon snakes
Peacocks overcome thirst
Bees are consuming poison
Waterbirds control their faculties
Lions are without any fear [7]

Owls are seeing at night
Vultures are in the know about jewels
Snakes are producing venom
Peacocks are ingesting poison
Ruddy shelducks know the future
Parrots are skilled with words [8]

Bumblebees erase their tracks
Animals and such roam through their own awareness
Geese separate milk from water
The sound of bees is very pleasant
Herons catch beings with tears
Snakes hear with their eyes [9]

Musk emerges from deer
Gunasas[84] smell with their eyes

Fish that live in the waters
End their life-force and effort
It would follow ill-disposed, repetitive
brahmans have supreme wisdom [10]

In all creatures such as tigers and so on,
the natural qualities emerging from
their past latent tendencies will arise
They do possess some worldly wisdom
but not the freedom that's not asceticism
Those emerging from past latent tendencies
are living in their own individual forms [11]

If just that much were wisdom,
animals would be free as well
Understanding this, abandon clinging
and engage in perfect wisdom,
through which genuine awakening
and genuine siddhis will emerge! [12]

A song by the ḍākinī Deity with the Sun Horse

For those who see what cannot be seen,
mind is free in itself—the dharmakāya
Leaving the stallion of the vāyus behind,
the rider of mind courses through the sky

Five stanzas by Kāṇhapa (Kṛṣṇa), the dark siddha

I pay homage to glorious Heruka

Through water becoming depleted, the lotus in the mud
withers away
With honey running away, there is no certainty where it went
By joining them with fire, roots, leaves, and trunk perish
Kṛṣṇa says, "Look at the laughter of the sense faculties!" [1]

Eating, drinking, hanging out, breaking branches, I wandered
Hey, this is my own karma, which is like caṇḍālī[85]
Something like an incessant girl burns the lotus
A hundred qualities are annihilated by a single flaw [2]

Through the ocean becoming depleted, the lotuses wither away
At that time, smoke comes forth from the ten gates
Worldly people are saying, "There is no Kṛṣṇa"
Kṛṣṇa dwells in the forest of the profound Mahāyāna [3]

Mind is empty and perfect in its native state
Though the skandhas are laughable, I have no regrets
Just as you don't see that butter exists within milk,
passion exists but is not seen by worldly people [4]

There is no worldly living or dying whatsoever
The one with such an experience is the yogī Kṛṣṇa
Even with his body parts withered away like a lotus,
Kṛṣṇa declares, "Why would I have died?" [5]

A song by the ḍākinī Śāntibhadrā

Hey! The true reality of mind cannot be described
The true reality of the basic ground cannot be conceived
The true reality of the dharma cannot be identified
The true reality of the path cannot be meditated on

A vajra song by Nāropa

I pay homage to the Bhagavan Mañjuvajra

Seized by the beguiling, poisonous snake
of these thoughts, your own mind
becomes fettered in just the ways
in which it keeps entertaining thoughts,
experiencing much meaningless suffering [1]

Through following delusion,
delusion will not be relinquished
The courageous with compassion
need to familiarize with suchness [2]

The mind will become free
according to its ways of analyzing
The many-headed, poisonous snake
of prajñā continues to devour me. [3]

The many-headed, poisonous snake of prajñā
is always nourished by the milk of samādhi
but killed by the mongoose of thoughts [4]

Prajñā's snake with its hundred heads
is constantly devouring Nāropa
Nobody can understand this—
only Nāropa himself gets it,
so ask Nāropa in person! [5]

A song by Dhobīpa, the eternal laundryman

Even if you may wash its stains for a long time,
the nature of charcoal will never become white
But naturally pure emptiness will become pure
The guru's instructions are the supreme natural launderer

A song by the ḍākinī Bhadrā

Look! Look at your own mind!
Looking, nothing is found; smash its root!
Make up branches however you please!
My thoughts are free in themselves

A Song on Connateness by Śāntadeva[86]

I pay homage to the genuine guru

In the empty forest, a flower bursts into bloom
This single flower has all kinds of colors
If this incomparable flower grows, it conquers all directions
Pluck this priceless flower! [1]

It has no roots and lacks any branches or leaves
Friends, behold this excellent bud as it conquers all directions!
If this incomparable flower grows, it conquers all directions
Pluck this priceless flower! [2]

Picking up its anthers, the illusionist
offers them to Kuliśeśvara,[87] the dharmadhātu
If this incomparable flower grows, it conquers all directions
Pluck this priceless flower! [3]

Examining the supreme [ecstasy] and cessational ecstasy,
seize and offer them with respect at the feet of the genuine guru!
If this incomparable flower grows, it conquers all directions
Pluck this priceless flower! [4]

A song by the yoginī Kaṅkarā

Nondual mind is like water poured into water
Don't impair its nature, let it be like an elephant!
No matter how the monkeys of experience may come up,
how could they pervade the sky of realization?

A Pith Instruction on Untying the Knots in the Yogī's Own Mind by Mitrayogī, the lord of miraculous powers

I pay homage to the bhagavān, noble Avalokiteśvara

AHO! That which is primordially unborn
is the cause that creates saṃsāra and nirvāṇa
Abiding nowhere else but in the center of your own heart,
it will be known from the mouth of the guru [1]

Hey, good sirs, listen to me!
The very cause that creates bondage
is the path that leads to freedom
Here, there is no bondage whatsoever [2]

In the vast city of illusion,
dream people enjoy themselves
At the time of enjoyment, there is no enjoyment
Thus appearances and mind should be known [3]

Diverse appearances are your own mind
They are like an assembly of snakes
Your own mind, being like Indra's bow,[88]
is effortless native luminosity [4]

Everything that arises is just that,
but it doesn't arise as anything at all
Hence, what has been born is unborn
This being unborn is the mode of being born [5]

Just as with the forms in a mirror, the sound of a vīṇā,[89]
bhikṣus, magical creations, and miraculous formations,
realize the characteristics of existence, nonexistence,
arising, ceasing, coming, and going [6]

Just like illusory horses and elephants,
appearances are dependent origination
True reality, just like the autumn sky,
is to be joined with luminosity's three dharmas [7]

AHO! The great king of yogīs
AHO! Neither bound nor free
AHO! No relinquishment, effortless
AHO! AHO! Great bliss [8]

In all beings without realization, independently
and through the power of great compassion,
nonreferential merit and wisdom
complete in all aspects shall be excellent [9]

A Dohā Treasure Song on the View of the Nature of True Reality by Lūhipa, the fish-gut eater

I pay homage to the glorious Heruka

So that the means for making the stainless mind,
view, conduct, and so on of the siddhas—the very embodiment
of the nectar of nonduality—a living experience will benefit all,
I pay homage to the sugatas and shall explain this[1]

It is neither being
nor arisen from nonbeing,
so who will realize
this kind of nature? [2]

This is what Lūhipa declares:
Something like that is amazing
Though it sports through the three realms' abodes,
the abode of true reality cannot be realized [3]

Neither its color, nor its type,
nor its shape can I realize
This kind of nature is not established
as an entity, so how can it be shown? [4]

This is what Lūhipa declares:
Something like that is amazing
Though it sports through the three realms' abodes,
the abode of true reality cannot be realized [5]

This is what Lūhipa declares:
How could I ask others?
The moon's reflection in the depths of water
cannot be realized as genuine or illusory [6]

This is what Lūhipa declares:
Something like that is amazing
Though it sports through the three realms' abodes,
the abode of true reality cannot be realized [7]

This is what Lūhipa declares:
How could I ask others?
Its nature cannot be realized [8]

A song by Vyālipa, the lucky alchemist

If you see the genuine guru, you see true reality
If you meditate in the sky's expanse, this is solitude supreme
If you realize phenomena, there is nothing discordant
If you drink the sky's milk, this will be your livelihood

A Dohā Treasure Song on True Reality by Thagana, the conman

I pay homage to Mañjuvajra

If examined, the entities of self and other do not exist—
they are like the dreams of a dumb fool
True reality is very difficult to realize,
just like a fool playing a game of dice [1]

This is what Thagana declares:
True reality is hard to express through words
Without discarding thoughts about appearance and emptiness,
how could liberation possibly be attained? [2]

If it is not understood that body, speech, and mind
are all three equal as true reality in the expanse,
true reality is very difficult to realize,
just like a fool playing a game of dice [3]

Things are hard to express through words
Even if phenomena are put into words,
are they established through mere words, or what? [4]

Without realizing the true reality of mind,
there is no realization of everything being one
The ultimate is very difficult to realize,
just like a fool playing a game of dice
This is what Thagana declares [5]

A song by Śyāmā

Within the vajra of immutable space,
magical displays of moving and shaking arise,
performing their functions for all kinds of beings
and vanishing within the space of being free in themselves

A Dohā Song on the True Reality of the Vāyus by Mahipa, the vain muscleman

I pay homage to nondual great bliss

The vāyus' palace of the stationary and moving
resides on the vajra seat of mind
Within profound emptiness,
hey, my darling, you the connate,
please be my witness! [1]

If this existence is shaking violently,
how will we meet again?
Hey, you beauty, you the connate,
please be my witness! [2]

If you are staying with me,
how would I search elsewhere?
For the one who wishes to be pulled out
from a ship that has already sunk,
hey, my darling, you the connate,
please be my witness! [3]

If this existence is shaking violently,
how will we meet again?
Even if I killed the assemblies
of the five families for your sake, [4]

I would not see your face
for even a single instant
Hey, my darling, you the connate,
please be my witness! [5]

If this existence is shaking violently,
how will we meet again?
Hey, you beauty, you the connate,
please be my witness! [6]

For your sake, I need
mudrā, without the slightest
thinking of brahmans of bad family
Hey, my darling, you the connate,
please be my witness! [7]

If this existence is shaking violently,
how will we meet again?
From him with a ship in the ocean,
the kāpālika[90] Kaṇha, [8]

Mahi received instructions
and severed the fetters of existence
Hey, you beauty, you the connate,
please be my witness! [9]

A song by Ekavajrā

In the volume of the sky of emptiness,
write the letters of self-aware wisdom,
formulate the instructions on all kinds of means,
and proclaim the teachings as an incessant stream!

A song by Saraha

I pay homage to the Buddha

Intertwined is the nature of emptiness and compassion
Emptiness exists inseparably without interruption
I see the empty yoginī,
milking, milking, and drinking the sky [1]

She does not see the sky's uniting with the sky
nor dwell on the plane of saṃsāric bondage
I see the empty yoginī,
milking, milking, and drinking the sky [2]

Such a yoginī moved out of her home that is her root
The great taste of compassion is stainless
I see the empty yoginī,
milking, milking, and drinking the sky [3]

Why should anybody else do what Saraha says?
Wandering day and night to milk the sky,
I see the empty yoginī,
milking, milking, and drinking the sky [4]

A song by Nairātmyā, selflessness embodied

Space, space—great equality
The sun, the sun—great primordial lucidity
Rivers, rivers—the uninterrupted flow
Rainbows—great bliss free in itself

A song by Śavaripa, the jungle hunter

In the dense jungle of ignorance
roams the deer of the duality of perceiver and perceived
Drawing the bow of both means and prajñā,
I shoot the single arrow of essential reality [1]

Its death is the dying of thoughts
Its flesh is consumed as nonduality
Its taste is experienced as great bliss—
the fruition of mahāmudrā is attained [2]

A vajra song by Virūkara, the stopper of the sun

I pay homage to the Buddha

Once the vajrayogī seizes his arrow,
knowing how to point out phenomena,
I shoot the arrow of the connate
without a target, not even a single thing to hit [1]

Please listen to this talk of the connate!
It's the arrow uniting with the entity of all
I shoot the arrow of the connate
without a target, not even a single thing to hit [2]

There exists no feeling apart from those
"This is through that" became nondual
I shoot the arrow of the connate
without a target, not even a single thing to hit [3]

No twenty cowries due as wages—
such a servant is Virūkara
I shoot the arrow of the connate
without a target, not even a single thing to hit [4]

A song by Vimalā

In primordially empty and void mind as such,
what's the point of meditating on being unborn?
In self-arising mental factors free in themselves,
what's the point of relinquishing thoughts?

A song by Ḍombi Heruka, the pregnant-tigress rider

I pay homage to the Buddha

Within many illusory forests here and there,
Ḍombi the fool wanders to kill deer
I see where the deer of wrong views is heading
Ḍombi shoots sharp arrows, entering right inside [1]

Five arrows I have, loosing them in a straight shot
Ḍombi remains holding the drawn bow string
I see where the deer of wrong views is heading
Ḍombi shoots sharp arrows, entering right inside [2]

With neither bow, nor string, nor reed, nor tip,
Ḍombi kills without a shade of doubt
I see where the deer of wrong views is heading
Ḍombi shoots sharp arrows, entering right inside [3]

With the five families' victors made my crown ornament
I bring the deer I killed right back to life
I see where the deer of wrong views is heading
Ḍombi shoots sharp arrows, entering right inside [4]

A song by the yoginī Mahāsiddhi

Don't meditate! Don't meditate! Don't meditate on mind!
Meditating on the mind is the whirl of delusion of thoughts
Through your thoughts, you are fettered in saṃsāra
Being free of the mind, there is nothing to meditate

A song by Mahāsukhata

Just as sesame oil pervades sesame seeds,
so the three realms are filled with Mañjuśrī's body
Knowing that, through cultivating the effortless yoga,
sing this dharma song of genuine great bliss! [1]

The nameless queen of all the sugatas
has all kinds of forms and embodies compassion
If you are together with her, all suffering is dispelled
Sing this dharma song of genuine great bliss! [2]

Just as the characteristic of space is space,
so is mind's dharmatā, the guru says
Unaware of this unsurpassable actuality, you cannot meditate
Sing this dharma song of genuine great bliss! [3]

By relying on the scriptures and the pith instructions,
just as the sun, a sun crystal, and cotton wool come together,
the fire of self-aware wisdom will blaze forth
Sing this dharma song of genuine great bliss! [4]

The dharma in texts and the wealth lying in the hands of others
are not the dharma or wealth—they're not there when you need them
Leap into the great wealth of the noble ones—your own mind!
Sing this dharma song of genuine great bliss! [5]

In all situations of happiness and suffering,
devote yourself day and night to Mañjuśrī, the guide of all,
the true reality that is like a wish-fulfilling jewel, bodhicitta
Sing this dharma song of genuine great bliss! [6]

A song by Taruparṇā

Who speaks this sound of an echo?
Who draws the reflections in a mirror?
Where do the spectacles in a dream unfold?
They don't exist anywhere—that's mind's natural state

A dharma song by Dīpaṃkaraśrījñāna, the scholar-siddha

I pay homage to the Buddha

If you know the fear of the destructive thieves of thoughts,
be a night watchman to guard the great wealth of discipline!
Hey, don't be lazy, act as the night watchman of the mind!
Due to the sleep of ignorance, the night of saṃsāra is long [1]

Hey, don't be lazy, act as the night watchman of the mind!
If you fall asleep, those thieves will enter your home
and will steal the great wealth of your discipline
Without the wealth of discipline, there is no samādhi
When this is missing, the sun will not shine [2]

Familiarizing with the sun of true reality, be a watchman!
Don't create any other trifling wealth for even an instant!
At that time, the sun of true reality will shine forth
Thus, at that point, this becomes the dawn of saṃsāra
Hey, don't be lazy, act as the night watchman of the mind! [3]

A song by Dignāga

Letting go of any activity is the pith instruction
If there is no wanting, this is realization
If there is nothing to accomplish, this is conduct
If there is nothing to express, this is experience
If there is nothing to be adopted or rejected, this is the fruition

A song by Kukkuripa, the one with a soft spot for dogs

Venerating buddhas and so on yields no meaning
If there is wanting and effort, this is not buddhahood
Experiencing the blessings of the genuine guru is splendid
It exists in ourselves in its entirety, but we don't see it

The View of Being Unbound and Letting Go by Kambala, the yogī wrapped in a black blanket

I pay homage to mother Vārāhī

On the racetrack of threefold existence here,
I, the bold one, continue racing on this track
I mounted the horses of the five sugatas
You do not find any rider in this world
who is galloping as audaciously as I
Racing, I tamed the wild horses of the three poisons [1]

I saddled them with the saddle of the four great gods
and put on the bridle of prajñā and means
You do not find any rider in this world
who is galloping as audaciously as I
Racing, I tamed the wild horses of the three poisons [2]

I gave them the food of the ten afflictions
and put them in the stable of the six views' center
You do not find any rider in this world
who is galloping as audaciously as I
Racing, I tamed the wild horses of the three poisons [3]

I brandish the sword of the guru's words
and ascend above the six pure abodes

You do not find any rider in this world
who is galloping as audaciously as I
Racing, I tamed the wild horses of the three poisons [4]

I galloped throughout the ten directions,
but the tracks of these horses are invisible
You do not find any rider in this world
who is galloping as audaciously as I
Racing, I tamed the wild horse of the three poisons [5]

A song by Līlabhadra

Though it exists in us, it is not recognized,
like a poor woman deceived about a treasure
I supplicate you to lift the lamp of compassion
for sentient beings who do not see true reality

A song by Jālandhara, the guru of gurus

If there is no wisdom, seeing is great
If there are no thoughts, lucidity is great
If there is no clinging, bliss is great
Not abiding anywhere, abiding is great

The View of Overcoming Mind's Thoughts by Lakṣmī, the "crazy" princess

I pay homage to Yamāntaka

Severing your head on fresh butter,
you break the blade of the ax
A frog will swallow an elephant
AHO! The woodcutter breaks into laughter [1]

AHO! Amazing, Mego,[91] hey!
Don't entertain doubts in your mind!
If you are stunned, Avadhūtīpa,
don't create thoughts in your mind! [2]

He didn't explain; this one did not understand
Flowers are growing out of the sky [3]

AHO! Amazing, Mego, hey!
Don't entertain doubts in your mind!
If you are stunned, Avadhūtīpa,
what's the point of a mind with doubts? [4]

AHO! If the child of a barren woman is born,
even a throne will break into dance
Since cotton wool is rare to obtain,
those wearing the sky as garment weep [5]

AHO! Amazing, Mego, hey!
What's the point of doubts in the mind?
If you are stunned, Avadhūtīpa,
don't entertain doubts in your mind! [6]

AHO! An elephant sits on a throne
that is supported by two bees
The blind leading the way—amazing!
The mute give speeches [7]

AHO! Amazing, Mego, hey!
Don't entertain doubts in your mind!
If you are stunned, Avadhūtīpa,
what's the point of a mind with doubts? [8]

A mouse chasing a cat—astounding!
Seeing that, amazement will arise
By seeing a crazy donkey,
even an elephant runs away [9]

AHO! Amazing, Mego, hey!
Don't entertain doubts in your mind!
If you are stunned, Avadhūtīpa,
what's the point of a mind with doubts? [10]

AHO! A famished monkey
gobbles down morsels of rock
AHO! The experience of the mind
cannot be expressed by anybody [11]

AHO! Amazing, Mego, hey!
Don't entertain doubts in your mind!
If you are stunned, Avadhūtīpa,
what's the point of a mind with doubts? [12]

A song by Durjayacandra

Just like searching the moon with a lamp,
thoughts themselves are nonthought
Just like searching space with space,
nonthought is beyond the mind

A song by Mekhalā, the elder severed-headed sister

Everything inner and outer is contained in the mind
If there is no clinging, this is equal taste
If there is no effort, this is meditation supreme
Nondual great bliss is perfect buddhahood

The View of Being Unbound by Kāṇhapa

I pay homage to the gurus

Haughtiness due to wealth, youth, or ancestry—
at the time when I will have perished,
not even a single one of those will appear [1]

How could there ever be a meeting
of what are called "me" and "you"?
Will a ship destroyed in the ocean
ever be reassembled, or what? [2]

Father, mother, children, and grandchildren
are like an audience come in order to watch a dance
Once the dancers have left, the show dissolves [3]

How could there ever be a meeting
of what are called "me" and "you"?
Will a ship destroyed in the ocean
ever be reassembled, or what? [4]

Be it at a market or in the streets,
on a mountain, a plain, or the banks of water—
at which place my body and speech will perish,
that is something I don't know [5]

How could there ever be a meeting
of what are called "me" and "you"?

Will a ship destroyed in the ocean
ever be reassembled, or what? [6]

This is what Kanapa[92] says:
I have no realization except this
Through coming and going, I was crushed [7]

How could there ever be a meeting
of what are called "me" and "you"?
Will a ship destroyed in the ocean
ever be reassembled, or what? [8]

A song by Prakāśā

If the actuality that cannot be understood is realized,
it becomes the narrative that cannot be expressed
Familiarizing with the actuality that cannot be thought,
the fruition that cannot be attained is emerging

Another song by Ḍombi Heruka

In the equality of saṃsāra and nirvāṇa free of discursiveness,
making effort and accomplishing are so utterly exhausting
To cling to the unobstructed nonduality of objects and mind
as something involving difference—how afflicted this is!
To cling to the dharmakāya of the nonduality of self and others
as something involving good and bad—how pitiful that is!

The Completion Stage of the Vajraḍākinī
by Vīṇāpa, the musical meditator

I pay homage to Vajravārāhī

While holding Vajrayoginī as your bow
and setting up all entities as the target,
Shoot with the arrow of nonduality—
meditation and something to meditate on are unseen! [1]

Through striking it, birth will not be observed
and the extremes of self and others are severed
Shoot with the arrow of nonduality—
neither meditation nor something to meditate on! [2]

By drawing the bow of emptiness,
the arrow that cannot miss strikes—
neither killing nor something to be killed
Shoot with the arrow of nonduality—
neither meditation nor something to meditate on! [3]

Having gathered the entirety of dharmatā
through the great miraculous display of space,
Shoot with the arrow of nonduality—
neither meditation nor something to meditate on! [4]

By Virū having cycled in this way,
from one all the way up to twenty,

without engaging in entities as anything at all,
empty syllables were provided as sustenance
Shoot with the arrow of nonduality—
neither meditation nor something to meditate on! [5]

A song by Javaripa, the petrifier

The three kāyas do not exist in outer objects—
it is out of the pellucid wisdom of awareness
that they dawn from within as mere reflections
You should not sully them through thoughts!

A song by the ḍākinī Queen of Saṃsāric Existence

Hey! If this king of self-awareness is seen,
all and everything is the path to liberation
If this very self-awareness is not realized,
there will never ever be any freedom

The Means to Calm Mind and Thinking
by Mekopa, the madman with a terrifying gaze

I pay homage to the glorious Heruka

Deer with fur in all kinds of colors
strike out with their legs and roam the four directions
Having hunted them down, I kill them in the sky [1]

In all respects, their own flesh
turns into an enemy for their own body
The hunter who is a bhusuku[93]
does not spare them for even an instant [2]

The doe calls out to the stag:
"If we stay in the forest, we will be fine
Once we step out of it, we are killed" [3]

In all respects, their own flesh
turns into an enemy for their own body
The hunter who is a bhusuku
does not spare them for even an instant [4]

The stag speaks like this to the doe:
"We have not done any harm to anybody,
and there is nothing at all to eat for us
If we haven't done any harm to anybody,
why would they shout, 'Kill them'?" [5]

In all respects, their own flesh
turns into an enemy for their own body
The hunter who is a bhusuku
does not spare them for even an instant [6]

Where grass and water are undamaged,
wherever they stay, they won't be hungry
Though I always searched for them,
I did not manage to find these two—
unfindable deer, the stag and the doe [7]

In all respects, their own flesh
turns into an enemy for their own body
The hunter who is a bhusuku
does not spare them for even an instant [8]

These running and walking deer—
their tracks are not to be found
Having hunted them down, I crush them in the sky's expanse [9]

The hunter who is a bhusuku
does not spare them for even an instant [10]

Another song by Lūhipa

Once the immutable native mind has become revealed,
searching for buddhahood with effort elsewhere is so tiresome,
like searching for a buffalo's tracks once that buffalo has been found
Since I know that there is no buddhahood, I'm free of a mind desiring it

A song by Bhasudhari

All sentient beings are sugatas
All appearances are the dharmakāya
All sense pleasures are mind's ornaments
All hosts of thoughts are great wisdom

A song by the ḍākinī Jñānavajrā

Hey! If you understand this magical display of all kinds
of appearances to be the perceiver and perceived of minding,
and you know that minding is empty of an essence of its own,
there is no need to search for the bliss of the expanse

A Pith Instruction on the View of Self-Aware Wisdom by Campaka, the flower-garden king

I pay homage to mother Nairātmyā

If self-aware wisdom were an object,
there would be no agent and no object
Without these, there would be no activity
How could three be nondual? [1]

If what is external were real,
due to conventional connection, it would be expressed as internal
If the seeming were self-awareness,
awareness through awareness would be unawareness [2]

If yogīs are aware of themselves,
the suffering of saṃsāra is overcome
By virtue of this convention, a nature
of things is not established, and they are stainless [3]

Since things are not established,
there is nothing else to be established for me
Therefore, I definitely do not exist

If words and their meanings were what is to be realized,
there would be no words or meanings in nature's actuality [4]

This yogī for whom entities are unestablished—
that is me—I am free from everything
In the freedom of duality, the darkness of ignorance is gone
Its absence represents stainless wisdom [5]

In this way, the yogī's awareness
frees the bondage of saṃsāra
By lying on the back, yoga arises
Be mindful of the body's meditative equipoise [6]

Open wide your eyes, offer up consciousness
By looking at the sphere of space,
there's nothing to be seen, nothing to grasp in the mind
By being free from thoughts about sides,
the faculties vanish and nonduality is accomplished [7]

A song by Śāntipa, the scholar whose student attained awakening before him

If resting, let be; if moving, let go!
Don't supervise; wander freely!
To seize anything deliberately is delusion
Look at the crow flying from the ship!

A song by the ḍākinī Wings of the Wind

Hey! Baseless phenomena are similar to dreams
Arising as appearances through conditions is like a reflection
Self-arising and self-subsiding resemble a bubble
The great freedom of any root is similar to space

A Pith Instruction on Pure View and Conduct by Śākyaśrībhadra, the mahāsiddha monk

I pay homage to the Bhagavān, the lion of the Śākyas

Just like in a dream, there is nothing outside
Just like in an illusion, there are no real referents
Just like with space, characteristics are lacking
All phenomena are natural luminosity [1]

Bodhicitta without coming, going, and remaining
is the expert in the vast welfare of sentient beings
The two accumulations' inseparability is the supreme path
Familiarize with the emptiness whose heart is compassion! [2]

A song by Anukirā, the yoginī of vajra recitation

Pellucid appearance-emptiness free of conditions
is not limited as the objects of the six collections
Within the native state without coming and going,
rest mind at ease in the gap between mindfulness and forgetting!

A Pith Instruction on the Liberation of Bondage by Mitrayogī

I pay homage to noble Avalokiteśvara

Hey!
The very cause that creates bondage
is the path that leads to freedom
Here, there is no bondage whatsoever
Freedom comes through that which binds [1]

Desire is pure as great bliss
Hatred blazes as luminosity's flame
Nescience is simply nonthought—
the three poisons are the effortless three kāyas [2]

A song by Kanakhalā, the younger severed-headed sister

Having donned the great armors,
through gem-like perseverance,
I steered the ship of my own mind,
sailing to the inner sanctum of this human corpse

The Self-Blessing of Glorious Connate Great Bliss by Śavaripa

I pay homage to the glorious Heruka

Hey, though the heart of practice, your own mind of great bliss,
has become associated with conditions under the sway of delusion,
the water of the ocean has the nature of transparent clarity,
while the nature of silt arises from adventitious conditions [1]

If it is let be uncontrived in its own place, it is the victor's mind
It arises here and now from relying on the guru's timely means
The king of means is that you need to let go of all doing [2]

A song by a group of ḍākinīs[94]

Usually, the small child of awareness is stuck in distraction
The appearances of delusion are such a great spectacle
The thieves of perceiver and perceived upset your head
States of mind with doubt and indecision are many

The watchmen of the remedies have little perseverance
Your armor of alertness and mindfulness is slack
There is the danger of losing the gem of mind as such
You, oh yogī, do not be distracted toward objects!

The cancer of the afflictions' five poisons invades
the queen of the space that is the changeless ground,
harmed by the nine evil spirit siblings of perceiver and perccived
and following the delusion of thoughts conditioned by good
and bad

Through inappropriate conduct due to attachment and aversion,
the chronic disease of perceiver and perceived rises from the depths,
and the well-being of your own body is lost and gone—
how pitiful are sentient beings full of delusion!
You, oh yogī, promote the welfare of beings!

Usually, the small child of the wisdom of mind
keeps listening to the lies of the five sense gates
There is the danger of being hurled into the abyss of the six classes
of beings

You, oh yogī, dismantle the clinging to duality!
The wild, moving mind of discursive thinking,
instead of lying down uncontrived and naked
in the palace that is the expanse of the ālaya,[95]
plays with the deception of illusory sense pleasures
by mingling with the friends of the five poisons

Being distracted toward the two objects of desire and hatred,
there is the danger of plunging into the abyss of the miserable realms
Close the doors of the five sense gates,
and lock the small child of mind in prison!
Stretch out on the bed of bliss, lucidity, and emptiness!
You, oh yogī, are headed for distraction!

In the river of birth, aging, sickness, and death,
the fools who cannot swim like to play around
While owning the ship of the freedoms and resources,
they do not rely on the ferryman of the guru lord,
but chatter away in the waves of nonvirtuous actions

Flee from the waves of suffering through the remedies!
Without being left behind in the mud of clinging,
pursue the dry shore of liberation as best as you can!
You, oh yogī, let go of your wanting!

On the tree trunk of the poison of desire,
the branches of adopting and rejecting spread,
the foliage of clinging grows in the ten directions,
the flowers of effortful accomplishing fly into the sky,
and the fruits of suffering keep plunging down
Picking them up, the monkey of cowardice eats them—
there is the danger of being bound in saṃsāra's jungle

Persons who do not cling to all kinds of things,
brandishing the weapon of immutable confidence,

knock down the tree of desire at its very foundation,
and carry away the unripe, dried-up fruits of the five poisons
Terminate the lethal power of this poison!
You, oh yogī, relinquish your wanting!

A peacock's wasting away and dying
is the payback for it seeing feathers as ornaments
Oh yogī, do not see the skandhas
of the unclean elements as yourself!

A bee's being stuck in the mud
is the payback for it being attached to sweet scents
Oh yogī, do not torment yourself with affection
for relatives with whom you have a transient connection!

A butterfly's being burned by fire
is the payback for it being attached to a lamp's shine
Oh yogī, do not entertain any clinging to
appearances of illusion-like objects as such!

A feathered creature's entrapment in a snare
is the payback for it pursuing sense pleasures as food
Oh yogī, do not entertain the hungry desire
for food with the iron hook of clinging!

With the mirror of the pure ālaya
polished by the six collections' awareness,
the clear reflections of the six objects appear
Childish beings without realization cling to them as entities,
experiencing the happiness and suffering of desire and hatred

The uncontrived ālaya, the dharmadhātu,
lacks clinging to the ceaseless six collections as such
The six objects are clear yet empty of essence
Childish beings clinging to entities can't help but weep

The wise are free of clinging to self-appearances as such
You, oh yogī, annihilate any clinging to them as such!

In the sky of the ground that cannot be identified,
the southern clouds of the afflictions' five poisons gather,
the thunder of the clinging to a self resounds,
and the continuous rain of all kinds of karma falls,
stirring the filthy swamp of saṃsāra with its attachment
Thus, the crops of the sufferings of the six beings grow

The sun of the awareness of superior insight
brings the sun of the expanse clearly to mind
The breeze of the mindfulness of equipoise and thereafter
dispels the southern clouds of discursive thinking in the expanse,
and the thunder of clinging to a self vanishes in its own place

The continuous rain of karma lacks any root
The sun dries up the filthy swamp of clinging
The seeds of the six classes of beings become parched
The unripe, dried-up harvest of suffering is carried away—
You, oh yogī, do not entertain any doubts!

The rightful prince who was cheated by his ministers
roamed as a beggar in lands without any friends,
soiled and barely making a living with tattered rags,
going unrecognized by either himself or others
A brahman expert in signs, realizing his pedigree,
queried this foolish young man with his insight

Entrust the basic nature to the lord of awareness,
extract it by washing it with the two pure accumulations,
adorn it with the wish-fulfilling jewel of the instructions,
place it on the jewel throne of realization,
and seize the royal seat of the buddhas of the three times!
You, oh yogī, must rely on the guru!

The deer of the mind without any physical support
roams the plain of the intermediate state through karma's force,
tormenting itself with the water of clinging's mirage
The six classes of beings die in the extreme state of saṃsāra

Mountains and valleys are full of the traces of their flesh and blood
Now, bind awareness without a physical support in space!
Not traveling on the surface of the six collections' conditions,
race across the vast plain of great luminosity!

Without entertaining any clinging to the river
of the mirage of the sense pleasures as such,
cut through the torment of wanting within!
Not traveling on the surface of the conditions of the six beings,
stretch out within the expanse of great equality!

In the native state of inconceivable mind,
the arrow maker of undistracted mindfulness
straightens it out as the uncontrived native essence
and cuts off the tip and the base of hope and fear

She wraps it in the attire of the four ecstasies,
inserts the arrowhead of connateness,
crafts the notch of means and prajñā,
attaches the feathers of the four moments,
and shoots it right at the clinging to a self

Pierce the heart of the wild pig of ignorance!
Sever the life-force nāḍī of perceiver and perceived!
Now, don't move around in this abode of saṃsāra!
You, oh yogī, must seize the fortress!

When objects appear as self-appearances without clinging,
the sense pleasures turn into the aids of the path
The colors of the lotus shine clearly in the mud
Oh yogī, sustain your experiences as you please!

With the stallion of the awareness of equality
not shackled with the chains of perceiver and perceived,
the bridle of clinging to self and other is loosened
Race across the plain without any direction as you please!

When the lunatic in whom experiences keep bubbling up
spontaneously is not put into the irons of the remedies,
he exits the house of fake discipline through the door
and freely wanders around in places as he pleases

With the garuḍa of the sky of realization
not attached to the food of philosophical systems
and not afraid of the abyss of delusion,
let him soar through the sky without bias!

With the wish-fulfilling jewel of the fruition
not tainted by the stains of hope and fear
and not left behind in the realm of wishful thinking,
persevere in facing the requests for all wants and needs!

Notes

1. Excerpted from *Do ha skor gsum gyi Ti ka 'bring po sems kyi rnam thar ston pa'i me long* by Karma Trinleypa (1456–1539); translation by Dzogchen Ponlop Rinpoche. The text preceding the quotation, as well as the paragraph that immediately follows it, also closely follows Karma Trinleypa's text.
2. Robinson 1979 and Dowman 1985.
3. Tib. *Nges don phyag rgya chen po'i rgya gzhung* (Khro ru klu sgrub rgya mtsho 2009).
4. Tib. Chos grags rgya mtsho; 1456–1539.
5. The Tengyur consists of the canonical Indian Buddhist texts by authors other than the Buddha that were translated into Tibetan.
6. I am currently working on translating the entire collection, whose six volumes will be published in a successive manner. In addition, the Tengyur contains a significant number of further Mahāmudrā works that are not included in the Karmapa's collection. Some of them will also be added to said forthcoming volumes.
7. For more details, see Robinson 1979 and Dowman 1985.
8. Skt. *nāḍī*, *vāyu*, and *bindu*. *Vāyu* (lit. "wind") is the proper Sanskrit term for what most people call *prāṇa* (while prāṇa is actually a specific one of the five main vāyus). In the songs, these practices are based mostly on the yoginī tantras (also known as "mother tantras" in Tibet), such as the Cakrasaṃvaratantra and the Hevajratantra.
9. Skt. *sahaja*, Tib. *lhan cig skyes pa*.
10. Skt. *nitya*, *ādhya*, Tib. *gnyug ma*.
11. Skt. *tattva*, Tib. *de (kho na) nyid*.

12. Skt. *yuganaddha*, Tib. *zung 'jug*.
13. Skt. **prākṛtajñāna*, Tib. *tha mal gyi shes pa*. This term, which later became such a hallmark of Tibetan Kagyü Mahāmudrā, was used in India much earlier. Though all the Indian works that use it exist only in Tibetan translations, the term is clearly understood in a number of them in the same sense as in later Tibetan Mahāmudrā texts that use it—as the ultimate, uncontrived nature of the mind. Gampopa's *Pith Instructions on the Two Armors* (Zhva dmar mi pham chos kyi blo gros 1997, 4:515) explains "ordinary mind" as "the first mind," which is unaltered by any opinions or philosophical systems.
14. For details on this threefold classification of Mahāmudrā, see Brunnhölzl 2014, 151–65.
15. Tib. Bcom ldan rig pa'i ral gri; 1227–1305.
16. See https://www.tbrc.org/#!rid=W3JT13307, subentry W3JT13307:008:0000.
17. Karma phrin las pa 1456–1539.
18. Karma phrin las pa phyogs las rnam rgal 2009, 8–10.
19. Jackson 2004, 10.
20. *Dohakoṣahṛdaya arthagītiṭīkā*, D2268, fol. 66a.4–5.
21. Schaeffer 2005, 97–98.
22. For more details, see 'Gos lo tsā ba gzhon nu dpal 1996 (841–66), Schaeffer 2005 (59–69 and 88–96), and my forthcoming introduction to the Seventh Karmapa's collection of Indian Mahāmudrā texts.
23. Tib. Mnga' ris jo stan (dan) chos kyi tshul khrims.
24. Tib. Gru shul pa.
25. Tib. (S)par phu ba blo gros seng ge. Born in the twelfth century, he was a studentof Chaba Chökyi Sengé (Phya pa chos kyi seng ge; 1109–69).
26. Tib. Ri mi 'babs pa bsod nams rin chen; 1362–1453.
27. Tib. 'Gos lo tsā ba gzhon nu dpal; 1392–1481.
28. Tib. Ras chung pa rdo rje grags; 1085–1161.
29. Tib. Dus gsum mkhyen pa; 1110–93.
30. Tib. Gling rje ras pa / Gling chen ras pa pad ma rdo rje; 1128–88.
31. Seven of Barpuwa's works on Saraha's dohās, the four works by the Third Karmapa, and a commentary and a summary by Lingjé Repa have recently been published in Tibetan (Grub thob gling ras, par phu ba blo gros seng ge, rgyal dbang karma pa rang byung rdo rje 2011). I intend to translate these texts, as well as Karma Trinlépa's commentaries on Saraha's three main dohās, in the future.
32. Tib. Nag tsho lo tsā ba tshul khrim rgyal ba; 1011–64.

33. Tib. Rma ban chos 'bar; ca. 1044–89.
34. Tib. Mtshur Jñānākara; eleventh century.
35. Tib. Gnyen dharma kī rti; eleventh century.
36. Tib. Ba reg thos pa dga'.
37. Tib. 'Brog mi jo sras ye shes rdo rje.
38. Tib. Nag po sher dad; eleventh/twelfth centuries.
39. Tib. Bla ma zhang brtson 'grus grags pa; 1123–93.
40. Tib. Khro phu lo tsā ba byams ba'i dpal; 1173–1236.
41. Tib. Gnubs tshul khrims shes rab; ca. twelfth century.
42. Tib. Glo bo lo tsā ba shes rab rin chen. Both Darpaṇācārya and Lowo Lotsāwa Sherab Rinchen lived in the thirteenth century.
43. Tib. Pha dam pa sangs rgyas; born in the eleventh century.
44. Tib. Zhva ma lo tsā ba seng ge rgyal po; eleventh century.
45. Tib. Mar pa lo tsā ba chos kyi blo gros; 1002/1012–1097/1100.
46. See Nālandā Translation Committee 1980 and 1986.
47. Tib. Mi la ras pa; 1040/1052–1123/1135.
48. Tib. Dpa' bo 'od gsal; K: no dates are known. The asterisk indicates that a name has been backtranslated from Tibetan. In addition, as pointed out by Kapstein (2000), three further works are related to this collection of texts: *King Kuñji's Banquet*, *A Garland of Gems* (a summary of the systems of tantric yoga and meditation taught by the eighty-four mahāsiddhas), and a commentary on the latter. These three texts are not contained in the Tengyur but in Jamgön Kongtrul's *Gdams ngag rin po che'i mdzod*. See also Dowman 1985, 384–88.
49. Eleventh/twelfth century.
50. Tib. Mi nyag lo tsā ba smon grub shes rab rin chen; eleventh/twelfth century.
51. Thirteenth century.
52. Tib. Yar klung lo tsā ba grags pa rgyal mtshan; 1242–1346. As Hahn (2016, 84) remarks, "the translations of this team are generally of a very poor quality."
53. Tib. Skor ni rū pa; 1062–1102.
54. Tib. Mar pa do pa chos kyi dbang phyug; 1042–1136.
55. This may be the Kṛṣṇa (also known as Balinācārya) who was a student of Nāropa and taught the *Guhyasamājatantra* in Tibet.
56. Tib. Me nag chen po.
57. Tib. Rgod tshang pa mgon po rdo rje; 1189–1258.
58. Tib. Gtsang pa rgya ras; 1161–1211.
59. Tib. Rang byung rdo rje; 1284–1339.

60. Tib. 'Brug pa kun legs; 1455–1529.
61. Tib. Klong chen rab 'byams pa dri med 'od zer; 1308–64.
62. Tib. Tshangs dbyangs rgya mtsho; 1683–1706.
63. Tib. Zhabs dkar tshogs drug rang grol; 1781–1851.
64. Tib. Dge 'dun chos 'phel; 1903–51.
65. Tib. O rgyan phrin las rdo rje; born 1985.
66. Tib. Chos rgyam drung pa rin po che; 1939–87.
67. Tib. Dil mgo mkhyen brtse; 1910–91.
68. Tib. Bdud 'joms rin po che; 1904–87.
69. Tib. Tshul khrims rgya mtsho rin poche; born 1934.
70. Tib. Rdzogs chen dpon slob rin po che; born 1965.
71. Translation by Ṭhānissaro Bhikkhu (2015, 5:2).
72. "Two-fingered wisdom" is an ancient Indian derogative meaning that women have very little intelligence.
73. Translation by Bhikkhu Bodhi 2000, 222–23.
74. Stanzas 10cd–12ab; my translation.
75. Stanzas 60–61 (lines 60c–61d correspond to lines 12c–13d of Kambala's *Garland of Light*); my translation.
76. Hess and Singh 1983, 100.
77. The translations of Meister Eckhart from German are mine.
78. Hillyer 1941, 598.
79. Kerouac 1997, 248.
80. Ginsberg 1984, 655.
81. Springsteen 2016, 186–87.
82. Over time, I have set some of the songs included here as well as others to melody with guitar accompaniment. MP3 recordings of these musical arrangements will be available online at some point in the future, downloadable for noncommercial use.
83. This was first translated in Brunnhölzl 2007, 137–38.
84. Tib. *gu na sa*; unidentified animal.
85. Skt. *caṇḍālī* can refer to a specific tantric practice with the body's subtle channels and energies, a passionate woman, a female member of a class of people in India generally considered to be outcastes and untouchables, a woman in the first day of her menses, the female energy located in the abdomen, and a plant whose root exudes a red milk that is used for the alchemistic fixing of mercury.
86. In a number of these songs, we find either the spelling Śāntadeva or Śāntideva.

However, it is not clear whether these always (or ever) refer to the same author, that is, the famous Śāntideva (eighth century) who also wrote the Bodhicaryāvatāra. As a mahāsiddha, Śāntideva is usually called Bhusuku (see Dowman 1985, 222–28).

87. This is an epithet of Vajradhara.
88. "Indra's bow" is an Indian expression for a rainbow.
89. The vīṇā is an Indian string instrument similar to a lute.
90. A kapālika is a skull-bearing yogī.
91. This appears to be a short form of Mekhalā, the elder severed-headed sister (see the song after the next one).
92. Another name for Kāṇhapa.
93. The three syllables of the term *bhusuku* refer to a lazy person who does nothing but eating (*bhu*), sleeping (*su*), and going out to the toilet (*ku*).
94. The following stanzas do not represent the entire song but are excerpts.
95. The Sanskrit term *ālaya* in these songs does not refer to the ālaya-consciousness that is the ground of saṃsāra but to the true nature of the mind or buddha nature.

Selected Bibliography

Bodhi, Bhikkhu. 2000. *The Connected Discourses of the Buddha: A Translation of the Saṃyutta Nikāya*. Somerville, MA: Wisdom Publications.

Brunnhölzl, Karl. 2007. *Straight From the Heart: Buddhist Pith Instructions*. Ithaca, NY: Snow Lion Publications.

———. 2014. *When the Clouds Part*. Boston: Snow Lion.

Davidson, Ronald. 2002. *Indian Esoteric Buddhism: A Social History of the Tantric Movement*. New York: Columbia University Press.

Dowman, Keith, trans. 1985. *Masters of Mahamudra: Songs and Histories of the Eighty-Four Buddhist Siddhas*. Albany: State University of New York Press.

Ginsberg, Allen. 1984. *Collected Poems: 1947–1980*. New York: Harper & Row.

'Gos lo tsā ba gzhon nu dpal. 1996. *The Blue Annals*. Translated by G. N. Roerich. Delhi: Motilal Banarsidass.

Grub thob gling ras, Par phu ba blo gros seng ge, and Rgyal dbang karma pa rang byung rdo rje. 2011. *Dmangs do ha'i rnam bshad de nyid gsal ba sogs dang / dmangs do ha'i 'grel bshad lhan skyes snang ba / btsun mo do ha'i 'grel bshad snying po rnam nges / rgyal po do ha'i 'grel bshad zla ba'i 'od zer sogs dang / dmangs do ha'i 'grel pa dri med sgron me sogs phyogs sgrig*. Sarnath, India: Vajra Vidya Institute Library.

Hess, Linda, and Shukdev Singh, trans. 1983. *The Bījak of Kabīr*. San Francisco: North Point Press.

Hillyer, Robert Silliman, ed. 1941. *The Complete Poetry and Selected Prose of John Donne and The Complete Poetry of William Blake*. New York: Modern Library.

Jackson, Roger R., trans. 2004. *Tantric Treasures: Three Collections of Mystical Verse from Buddhist India*. Oxford: Oxford University Press.

Kapstein, Matthew. 2000. "King Kuñji's Banquet." In *Tantra in Practice*, edited by David G. White, 52–71. Princeton, NJ: Princeton University Press.

Karma phrin las pa phyogs las rnam rgyal. 2009. *Do ha skor gsum gyi tshig don gyi rnam bshad sems kyi rnam thar gsal bar ston pa'i me long / btsun mo do ha'i ṭī ka 'bring po sems kyi rnam thar ston pa'i me long / rgyal po do ha'i ṭī ka 'bring po sems kyi rnam thar ston pa'i me long*. Sarnath, India: Vajra Vidya Institute Library.

Kerouac, Jack. 1997. *Some of the Dharma*. Toronto: Viking.

Khro ru klu sgrub rgya mtsho, ed. 2009. *Phyag rgya chen po'i rgya gzhung*. In *Nges don phyag chen rgya gzhung dang bod gzhung*. Vols. 1–6. Chengdu, China: Si khron mi rigs dpe skrun khang.

Linrothe, Robert N., ed. *Holy Madness: Portraits of Tantric Siddhas*. New York, Chicago: Rubin Museum of Art and Serindia Publications.

Nālandā Translation Committee, trans. 1980. *The Rain of Wisdom*. Boulder, CO: Shambhala Publications.

———. 1986. *The Life of Marpa the Translator*. Boston: Shambhala Publications.

Robinson, James Burnell. 1979. *Buddha's Lions: The Lives of the Eighty-Four Siddhas*. Berkeley: Dharma Publishing.

Schaeffer, Kurtis Rice. 2005. *Dreaming the Great Brahmin*. Oxford: Oxford University Press.

Schroeder, Ulrich von. 2006. *Empowered Masters: Tibetan Wall Paintings of Mahasiddhas at Gyantse*. Chicago: Serindia Publications.

Springsteen, Bruce. 2016. *Born to Run*. New York: Simon & Schuster.

Ṭhānissaro Bhikkhu. 2015. *Poems of the Elders: An Anthology from the Theragāthā and Therīgāthā*. Published on www.dhammatalks.org. https://www.dhammatalks.org/Archive/Writings/Ebooks/PoemsoftheElders_181215.pdf.

White, David Gordon. 1996. *The Alchemical Body: Siddha Traditions in Medieval India*. Chicago: University of Chicago Press.

Zhwa dmar mi pham chos kyi blo gros, ed. 1997. *Nges don phyag rgya chen po'i khrid mdzod*. 13 vols. New Delhi: Rnam par rgyal ba dpal zhwa dmar ba'i chos sde.

About the Author

KARL BRUNNHÖLZL, MD, PHD, was originally trained as a physician. He received his systematic training in Tibetan language and Buddhist philosophy and practice at the Marpa Institute for Translators, founded by Khenpo Tsultrim Gyamtso Rinpoche, as well as the Nitartha Institute, founded by Dzogchen Ponlop Rinpoche. Since 1989 he has been a translator and interpreter from Tibetan and English. Karl Brunnhölzl is a senior teacher and translator in the Nalandabodhi community of Dzogchen Ponlop Rinpoche, as well as at Nitartha Institute. Living in Seattle, he is the author and translator of numerous texts. Currently, he is working on a complete translation of the Seventh Karmapa's compilation of Indian Mahāmudrā works, from which this book draws.

What to Read Next from Wisdom Publications

A Lullaby to Awaken the Heart
Samantabhadra's Aspiration Prayer and Its Tibetan Commentaries
Karl Brunnhölzl

"Among translators, Brunnhölzl is unsurpassed in his knowledge of Tibetan and Sanskrit Buddhist literature. His deep practice experience brings the meaning and intent of texts to life. In *A Lullaby to Awaken the Heart* he brilliantly presents the teachings in *The Aspiration Prayer of Samantabhadra*, a gateway into the profundity of the Dzogchen teachings."—Andy Karr, author of *Contemplating Reality*

A Song for the King
Saraha on Mahamudra Meditation
Khenchen Thrangu Rinpoche

"A lively commentary [on] a poetic classic of Buddhist literature. Editor Michele Martin has supplemented Thrangu Rinpoche's lucid commentary with notes and appendices that make the book as accessible for novices as it is rewarding for experienced practitioners and scholars."—*Buddhadharma*

Drinking the Mountain Stream
Songs of Tibet's Beloved Saint, Milarepa
Translated by Lama Kunga Rinpoche and Brian Cutillo

Jetsun Milarepa, Tibet's renowned and beloved saint, is known for his penetrating insights, wry sense of humor, and ability to render any lesson into spontaneous song. His songs and poems exhibit the bold, inspirational leader as he guided followers along the Buddhist path.

Essentials of Mahamudra
Looking Directly at the Mind
Khenchen Thrangu Rinpoche

"Makes the practice of mahamudra, one of the most advanced forms of meditation, easily accessible to Westerners' everyday lives. A wonderful way of bringing us to the path."—*Mandala*

Mahāmudrā
The Moonlight—Quintessence of Mind and Meditation
Dakpo Tashi Namgyal

"This updated edition of an English translation of a great classic for mastering mind and meditation comes recommended by the Dalai Lama.... A fundamentally valuable addition to one's Dharma library."—*Mandala*

The Mind of Mahāmudrā
Advice from the Kagyü Masters
Translated by Peter Alan Roberts

"Quite simply, the best anthology of Tibetan Mahāmudrā texts yet to appear."—Roger R. Jackson, author of *Mind Seeing Mind*

About Wisdom Publications

Wisdom Publications is the leading publisher of classic and contemporary Buddhist books and practical works on mindfulness. To learn more about us or to explore our other books, please visit our website at wisdomexperience.org or contact us as the address below.

Wisdom Publications
199 Elm Street
Somerville, Massachusetts 02144 USA

We are a 501(c)(3) organization, and donations in support of our mission are tax deductible.

Wisdom Publications is affiliated with the Foundation for the Preservation of the Mahayana Tradition (FPMT)